PRAYER: A BAH[...]

Prayer
A Bahá'í Approach

by

William and Madeline Hellaby

GEORGE RONALD
OXFORD

GEORGE RONALD, Publisher
46 High Street, Kidlington, Oxford, OX5 2DN

Reprinted 1990

British Library Cataloguing in Publication Data

Hellaby, William
  Prayer: A Bahá'í approach.
  1. Bahais   2. Prayer
  I. Title   II. Hellaby, Madeline
  297.894'3   BP380

  ISBN 0-85398-212-0
  ISBN 0-85398-213-9 Pbk

Printed in England

Contents

PART II: PRAYER AS A LIVING REALITY
by
Madeline Hellaby

Foreword

In their Message of March 1981, addressed to the Bahá'ís of the world, the Universal House of Justice has said we must never forget that 'our service is a spiritual one'. One of the most obvious aids to spirituality is prayer. As a community – and indeed as individuals within that community – it can be safely said that we do not pray enough. This may perhaps partly be because we don't know a great deal about the subject.

Over the centuries, literally thousands of books have been written about prayer, many by dedicated and saintly people whose works have helped countless numbers of more ordinary souls to understand the meaning of prayer and to put prayer at the centre of their lives.

In the Bahá'í Faith we are immeasurably fortunate in the number of our revealed prayers – prayers whose potency is therefore far greater than anything we can phrase for ourselves. There is a vast reservoir of power here waiting for us to tap; an ocean of utterance in whose depths we must plunge if we are to obtain the pearls of great price contained therein.

The following notes are only the beginnings of study of

this inexhaustible subject. They were first prepared for a seminar in Northern Ireland, then rearranged for some sessions at Summer School. They have now been rearranged again for general study. The first part is especially geared to the compilation from the Universal House of Justice called *The Importance of Prayer, Meditation and the Devotional Attitude* and the friends would find it helpful to have this booklet alongside them at the same time.

Many non-Bahá'í writers have contributed profound and helpful insights into the subject of prayer and the second half of these notes owes a great deal to an inspiring book by Dr Harry Emerson Fosdick called *The Meaning of Prayer* – now regrettably out of print.

William and Madeline Hellaby

January 1984

PART I

Prayer – Man's Link with God

by

William Hellaby

I

The Need for Prayer

Man's relationship to God

Why do you and I need to pray? 'Abdu'l-Bahá tells us
why. He tells us we have been created by a loving God.
Every breath, every heart-beat, every thought, every
aspiration depends upon Him. We can make no progress
without His help and so the unknowable God has unveiled
His beauty in the Person of His divine Messenger, His
Son, the High Prophet for this age.

Know that the conditions of existence are limited to the
conditions of servitude, of prophethood and of Deity . . .
As the divine bounties are endless, so human perfections are
endless . . .
But for every being there is a point which it cannot overpass –
that is to say, he who is in the condition of servitude, however
far he may progress in gaining limitless perfections, will never
reach the condition of Deity . . . A mineral cannot gain the
vegetable power. Also in a flower, however far it may progress
in the vegetable kingdom, no power of the senses will appear
. . .
. . . Peter cannot become Christ. All that he can do is, in the
condition of servitude, to attain endless perfections . . . [1]

Our relationship to God is one of servitude but it is a relationship which begins in the heart of God. In the *Hidden Words* of Bahá'u'lláh we read:

Veiled in My immemorial being and in the ancient eternity of My essence, I knew My love for thee; therefore I created thee, have engraved on thee Mine image and revealed to thee My beauty.[2]

The Old Testament speaks in the same language: 'So God created man in His own image.'[3] But He did not create us and then leave us alone. Indeed, if He did not reach out we would be lost. The Books of God down the ages confirm that He manifested His Word:

For God so loved the world that He gave His only Son . . .[4]

In the beginning was the Word . . . And the Word became flesh and dwelt among us . . .[5]

So the divine-human drama begins with God reaching out in love to us.

The relationship between the soul of man and the Word of God

In creating us He has implanted in us a hunger and thirst for His spirit:

I loved thy creation, hence I created thee. Wherefore, do thou love Me, that I may name thy name and fill thy soul with the spirit of life.[6]

There is no peace for thee save by renouncing thyself and turning unto Me . . .[7]

We cannot raise ourselves above the crude materialism of society without cultivating that mystic feeling which unites us with God. We need to come into God's Presence in prayer so that He may fill our souls with the 'spirit of life' and the divine seeds may stir into growth. The Universal House of Justice wrote to us in March 1981:

Beloved friends, the world moves deeper into the heart of darkness as its old order is rolled up. Pursuing our objectives with confidence, optimism, and an unshakeable resolve, we must never forget that our service is a spiritual one. Mankind is dying for lack of true religion and this is what we have to offer to humanity. It is the love of God, manifest in the appearance of Bahá'u'lláh, which will feed the hungry souls of the world and eventually lead the peoples out of the present morass into the orderly, uplifting, and soul-inspiring task of establishing God's Kingdom on earth.[8]

You and I are members of Bahá'u'lláh's World Order and only if we feed our souls with spiritual nourishment through the practice of prayer shall we have anything worthwhile to bring into this Kingdom.

Nearly fifty years ago the Guardian wrote about this:

The problem with which you are faced is one which concerns and seriously puzzles many of our present-day youth. How to attain spirituality is indeed a question to which every young man and woman must sooner or later try to find a satisfactory answer. It is precisely because no such satisfactory answer has been given or found, that the modern youth finds itself bewildered, and is being consequently carried away by the materialistic forces that are so powerfully undermining the foundations of man's moral and spiritual life.

Indeed, the chief reason for the evils now rampant in society is the lack of spirituality. The materialistic civilization of our age has so much absorbed the energy and interest of mankind that people in general do no longer feel the necessity of raising themselves above the forces and conditions of their daily material existence. There is not sufficient demand for things that we should call spiritual to differentiate them from the needs and requirements of our physical existence.

The universal crisis affecting mankind is, therefore, essentially spiritual in its causes. The spirit of the age, taken on the whole, is irreligious. Man's outlook on life is too crude and materialistic to enable him to elevate himself into the higher realms of the spirit.

It is this condition, so sadly morbid, into which society has fallen, that religion seeks to improve and transform. For the core of religious faith is that mystic feeling which unites man with God. This state of spiritual communion can be brought about and maintained by means of meditation and prayer. And this is the reason why Bahá'u'lláh has so much stressed the importance of worship. It is not sufficient for a believer merely to accept and observe the teachings. He should, in addition, cultivate the sense of spirituality which he can acquire chiefly by means of prayer. The Bahá'í Faith, like all other Divine Religions, is thus fundamentally mystic in character. Its chief goal is the development of the individual and society, through the acquisition of spiritual virtues and powers. It is the soul of man which has first to be fed. And this spiritual nourishment prayer can best provide. Laws and institutions, as viewed by Bahá'u'lláh, can become really effective only when our inner spiritual life has been perfected and transformed. Otherwise religion will degenerate into a mere organization, and becomes a dead thing.

The believers, particularly the young ones, should, therefore, fully realize the necessity of praying. For prayer is absolutely indispensable to their inner spiritual development, and this, as already stated, is the very foundation and purpose of the religion of God.[9]

Prayer, alone, strengthens this 'mystic bond':

Immerse yourselves in the ocean of My words, that ye may unravel its secrets, and discover all the pearls of wisdom that lie hid in its depths. Take heed that ye do not vacillate in your determination to embrace the truth of this Cause – a Cause through which the potentialities of the might of God have been revealed, and His sovereignty established. With faces beaming with joy, hasten ye unto Him. This is the changeless Faith of God, eternal in the past, eternal in the future. Let him that seeketh, attain it; and as to him that hath refused to seek it – verily, God is Self-Sufficient, above any need of His creatures.[10]

Plunge into this ocean, search in its depths and see what treasures of wisdom and power God will give you. This passage conjures up the image of the pearl diver – and by the way, I was intrigued to find, in my Biblical Concordance, that the finest pearls are fished up in the Persian Gulf! You know that Jesus spoke about pearls too:

The Kingdom of heaven is like a merchant in search of fine pearls, who, on finding one pearl of great value, went and sold all that he had and bought it.[11]

Together we are seeking for something which will transform our own souls and through us this tragic world.

The Word of God and the Covenant

Now in relation to our need to immerse ourselves in Bahá'u'lláh's Words there is a verse which challenges our thought:

Recite ye the verses of God every morning and evening. Whoso reciteth them not hath truly failed to fulfil his pledge to the Covenant of God and His Testament and whoso in this day turneth away therefrom, hath indeed turned away from God since time immemorial. Fear ye God, O concourse of My servants.[12]

That shows how important this duty is. Like the words in the 'Tablet of Aḥmad', 'he who turns away from this Beauty hath also turned away from the Messengers of the past'.[13] Ah, but there is a marvellous balance in the Faith:

Take heed lest excessive reading and too many acts of piety in the daytime and in the night season make you vainglorious. Should a person recite but a single verse from the Holy Writings in a spirit of joy and radiance, this would be better for him than reciting wearily all the Scriptures of God, the Help in Peril, the Self-Subsisting. Recite ye the verses of God in such measure that ye be not overtaken with fatigue or boredom. Burden not your souls so as to cause exhaustion and weigh them down, but rather endeavour to lighten them, that they may soar on the wings of revealed Verses unto the dawning-place of His signs. This is conducive to nearer access unto God, were ye to comprehend.[14]

Maybe there have been times when we have felt tired of reading – and then we have felt guilty; but Bahá'u'lláh reassures us that it is not the number of words we recite; it is the spirit that matters. Even one verse, even 'Alláh-u-Abhá' cried out with joy is acceptable to Him:

He feels more emphasis should be laid on the importance and power of prayer, including the use of The Greatest Name, but not over-emphasizing. It is the spirit behind the words which is really important.[15]

'Pray as you can,' wrote Dom John Chapman, 'don't try to pray as you can't.' But he also said, 'The less you pray, the worse it goes.'[16]

Renunciation and detachment

Regarding the inner spirit of our prayers or meditations, Bahá'u'lláh uses two interesting words; they are 'renunciation' and 'detachment'. The Latin root of 'attachment' is 'tacca', meaning a nail or tack. It suggests that we are firmly pinned to this world by the nail of materialism. We can free ourselves only by renunciation, that is, the denial of self-will and the adoption of God's Will. In the *Kitáb-i-*

Íqán Bahá'u'lláh talks of 'those people who, despite the love and yearning for truth which they profess, curse the followers of Truth when once He hath been made manifest'.[17] If we take our self-will with us into prayer we are in danger of being hypocritical, that is, paying lip-service to virtue but firmly pinned to the ground of self-will:

> . . . The wine of renunciation must needs be quaffed, the lofty heights of detachment must needs be attained, and the meditation referred to in the words 'One hour's reflection is preferable to seventy years of pious worship' must needs be observed, so that the secret of the wretched behaviour of the people might be discovered, those people who, despite the love and yearning for truth which they profess, curse the followers of Truth when once He hath been made manifest.[18]

How do we lift up our eyes and ascend 'the lofty heights of detachment'? We cannot escape from this plight except by meditating on the Words of the Manifestation until we reach a point of embracing His Law with a radiant heart. It is very difficult, isn't it? To acquiesce is difficult enough but how do we acquiesce radiantly? Bahá'u'lláh tells us to use the 'burnish of the spirit': 'Cleanse thy heart with the burnish of the spirit.'[19] To burnish is to polish by friction. It is a spiritual exercise that may be hard, painful. Of course, the athlete spends hours, days, years, preparing his body. The scholar must accept his disciplines. Prayer is the burnish, the discipline of the spirit.

Purify and clarify thy spiritual nostrils

Let us change the metaphor dramatically and use a homely, almost humorous, one of 'Abdu'l-Bahá's. He says:

. . . purify and clarify thy spiritual nostrils from every worldly moisture, then thou wilt inhale the holy fragrances diffusing from the merciful gardens of these worlds . . . [20]

He seems to be talking of those temporary spiritual illnesses we all experience; you might call them the childish ailments of the spirit. We catch a cold, a depression clouds our spirit; the fragrances and colours of the garden are meaningless. In Persian, I understand, the word 'garden' is almost synonymous with 'paradise'. One thinks of the Garden of Eden and, more appropriately in our case, the Garden of Riḍván. Bahá'u'lláh said of the time He was there, 'all created things were immersed in the sea of purification'.[21] He also said, 'Guide . . . the people unto the garden of delight.'[22]

The journey from the material world to the spiritual one

We are all walking towards that garden of delight whose fragrances can give us joy even in this world; but we may have many difficult times. Life is continuous. Day by day we make decisions. Some help us along the road to spiritual happiness; others enmesh us in selfish, worldly pursuits. We may cease to pray; the mirror of our soul may get clouded; our spiritual nostrils may get blocked. Spiritual life is never static. Either we are slipping backwards or moving towards the spiritual world. Our perceptions of sight, hearing and smell need to be keen, 'so that we can see the signs and traces of God's spirit in everything'.[23] That marvellous passage in the *Kitáb-i-Íqán* explains it in a way that only a Manifestation of God can:

Only when the lamp of search, of earnest striving, of longing desire, of passionate devotion, of fervid love, of rapture, and

ecstasy, is kindled within the seeker's heart, and the breeze of
His loving-kindness is wafted upon his soul, will the darkness
of error be dispelled, the mists of doubts and misgivings be
dissipated, and the lights of knowledge and certitude envelop
his being. At that hour will the mystic Herald, bearing the
joyful tidings of the Spirit, shine forth from the City of God
resplendent as the morn, and, through the trumpet-blast of
knowledge, will awaken the heart, the soul, and the spirit from
the slumber of negligence. Then will the manifold favours and
outpouring grace of the holy and everlasting Spirit confer such
new life upon the seeker that he will find himself endowed with
a new eye, a new ear, a new heart, and a new mind. He will
contemplate the manifest signs of the universe, and will
penetrate the hidden mysteries of the soul. Gazing with the eye
of God, he will perceive within every atom a door that leadeth
him to the stations of absolute certitude. He will discover in all
things the mysteries of divine Revelation and the evidences of
an everlasting manifestation.

I swear by God! Were he that treadeth the path of guidance
and seeketh to scale the heights of righteousness to attain unto
this glorious and supreme station, he would inhale at a distance
of a thousand leagues the fragrance of God, and would perceive
the resplendent morn of a divine Guidance rising above the
day-spring of all things. Each and every thing, however small,
would be to him a revelation, leading him to his Beloved, the
Object of his quest. So great shall be the discernment of this
seeker that he will discriminate between truth and falsehood
even as he doth distinguish the sun from shadow. If in the
uttermost corners of the East the sweet savours of God be
wafted, he will assuredly recognize and inhale their fragrance,
even though he be dwelling in the uttermost ends of the West.
He will likewise clearly distinguish all the signs of God – His
wondrous utterances, His great works, and mighty deeds –
from the doings, words, and ways of men, even as the jeweller
who knoweth the gem from the stone, or the man who
distinguisheth the spring from autumn and heat from cold.
When the channel of the human soul is cleansed of all worldly
and impeding attachments, it will unfailingly perceive the

breath of the Beloved across immeasurable distances, and will, led by its perfume, attain and enter the City of Certitude.[24]

How beautiful and profound! No wonder Bahá'u'lláh described His Revelation as an ocean!

Prayer is natural to the spirit of man

'When the channel of the human soul is cleansed of all worldly attachments, it will unfailingly perceive . . . the Beloved.' Prayer is natural to the spirit of man:

If one friend feels love for another, he will wish to say so. Though he knows that the friend is aware that he loves him, he will still wish to say so . . . God knows the wishes of all hearts. But the impulse to pray is a natural one, springing from man's love to God.

Prayer need not be in words, but rather in thought and attitude. But if this love and this desire are lacking, it is useless to try to force them. Words without love mean nothing. If a person talks to you as an unpleasant duty, with no love or pleasure in his meeting with you, do you wish to converse with him?[25]

When our heart is full we spontaneously express our love for a friend or a lover. We feel we must show it in words or attitude or even in a glance or smile. When we fall in love with Bahá'u'lláh we have the privilege of telling Him of our love by using His 'most august and precious speech'.[26]

Prayer reveals the beauty of the Divine Countenance

In one of His Writings 'Abdu'l-Bahá seems to talk of prayer as revealing the beauty of the Divine Countenance. It is in a Tablet written to a lady and He uses these words:

O thou who hast bowed thyself down in prayer before the Kingdom of God! Blessed art thou, for the beauty of the divine Countenance hath enraptured thy heart, and the light of inner wisdom hath filled it full, and within it shineth the brightness of the Kingdom. Know thou that God is with thee under all conditions, and that He guardeth thee from the changes and chances of this world and hath made thee a handmaid in His mighty vineyard . . . [27]

What does this mean? In a way, our readings from the *Kitáb-i-Íqán* have already answered this question; but I do wonder whether the lady to whom this Tablet was written had ever seen 'Abdu'l-Bahá. Some who have seen Him have been so enraptured that they have fallen at His feet. But it means much more than that! In the Book of Revelation, St. John the Divine says that when Jesus returns, 'Behold, He cometh with clouds; and every eye shall see him, . . .'[28] 'Abdu'l-Bahá commented about that, 'Every eye, yes . . .'[29] Like Jesus, He emphasised that the eye must be open. You remember that Jesus said, 'their eyes they have closed, lest they should perceive with their eyes . . .'[30] Bahá'u'lláh, speaking about the coming of Christ, of Muḥammad and of Himself, tells how the people 'turned away from His face – the face of God Himself'.[31] Clearly, He is talking about our inner eyes. If they are open we see the world as God's Kingdom, His Vineyard. The glamour and cares of the world fall into place and we have discovered an ultimate security.

Why we pray

Let us look again at 'Abdu'l-Bahá's words about our nature and why we pray. He speaks of each one of us as a trinity with the three aspects of body, mind and spirit. All aspects need food. Few deny the body's need though we read of the occasional ascetic who reduced his food to the proverbial straw. Greater numbers neglect to feed their minds. But vast numbers, in practice, deny the need for spiritual food and we see the result; the collapse of standards everywhere as the 'world moves deeper into the heart of darkness';[32] and note the craving for religion in formally atheistic countries, where churches are filled to overflowing. 'Deliver your souls, O people, from the bondage of self . . . Remembrance of Me cleanseth all things from defilement.'[33] In His Light the world of nature, our companions, the everyday events of our lives, become signposts to God and not barriers blocking out this Light. Turning the soul heavenward illumines all the worlds enfolded in man:

When man allows the spirit, through his soul, to enlighten his understanding, then does he contain all creation . . . But on the other hand, when man does not open his mind and heart to the blessing of the spirit, but turns his soul towards the material side, towards the bodily part of his nature, then is he fallen from his high place and he becomes inferior to the inhabitants of the lower animal kingdom.[34]

When we look heavenward to Bahá'u'lláh's Revelation the chains of self gradually fall away. We do not lose the homely gifts of earth: we see them with a new eye and use them in a new way. 'Abdu'l-Bahá's words, 'then does he contain all creation' are interesting. In Some Answered Questions, He tells us that physical evolution has reached its highest point in man.[35] Bahá'u'lláh says the same: 'I . . . have ordained for thy training every atom in existence and the essence of all created things.'[36] Spiritual development goes on and without looking beyond the world of nature to the world of God's Revelation, we cannot discover that we are children of God and that the purpose of life is to grow spiritually. The spiritual man is one who has fallen in love with God and prayer is the language of love for God:

In the highest prayer, men pray only for the love of God, not because they fear Him or hell, or hope for bounty or heaven . . . When a man falls in love with a human being, it is impossible for him to keep from mentioning the name of his beloved. How much more difficult is it to keep from mentioning the Name of God when one has come to love Him . . . The spiritual man finds no delight in anything save in commemoration of God.[37]

The command to pray

If this is true, one might ask, why should Bahá'u'lláh command us to pray? For example, He says, 'Forget all save Me and commune with My spirit. This is the essence of My command, therefore turn unto it.'[38] Of course, over the years, the laws governing our physical bodies have been gradually discovered and these laws make imperative demands that we should breathe clean air, cleanse ourselves with water and eat good food. Likewise God's Messengers have gradually revealed spiritual laws which demand our obedience if we want spiritual health. If you want to be physically clean – wash! If you want to be spiritually clean – use prayer, the water of life. St. Teresa of Jesus (also known as St. Teresa of Avila), the Spanish mystic and saint, has written some profound works on prayer and some of her words about the imperative need to pray are interesting. In her autobiography she writes:

Whenever I entered the oratory I used to feel so depressed that I had to summon up all my courage to make myself pray at all. (People say that I have little courage, and it is clear that God has given me much more than to most women, only I have made bad use of it.) In the end, the Lord would come to my help. Afterwards, when I had forced myself to pray, I would find that I had more tranquillity and happiness than at certain other times when I had prayed because I had wanted to.

Now if the Lord bore for so long with such a wicked creature as I – and it is quite clear that it was in this way that all my wrong was put right – what other person, however wicked he may be, can have any reason for fear?[39]

When and how we should pray

Now Bahá'u'lláh makes it easier for us by giving some guidance as to when and how we should pray. For example, there are the Obligatory Prayers and there is the injunction to pray morning and evening. And this brings us to the important question of how to concentrate our minds. Shoghi Effendi writes:

While praying it would be better to turn one's thoughts to the Manifestation as He continues, in the other world, to be our means of contact with the Almighty. We can, however, pray directly to God Himself.[40]

But he writes elsewhere to an individual believer:

If you find you need to visualize someone when you pray, think of the Master. Through Him you can address Bahá'u'lláh. Gradually try to think of the qualities of the Manifestation, and in that way a mental form will fade out, for after all the body is not the thing. His Spirit is there and is the essential, everlasting element.[41]

This is really the way the Christian approaches God; that is, 'through Jesus Christ, our Lord'. Well, being human, we need to focus our minds on something and indeed, Shoghi Effendi says, in a letter to an individual believer, 'our prayers would certainly be more effective and illuminating if they are addressed to Him [God] through His Manifestation, Bahá'u'lláh'.[42] But there is no rigidity here. We can focus our thoughts on Bahá'u'lláh, 'Abdu'l-Bahá or even the Guardian and ask them to intercede, as long as we understand their respective stations:

In regard to your question: we must not be rigid about praying; there is not a set of rules governing it; the main thing is we must start out with the right concept of God, the Manifestation, the Master, the Guardian – we can turn, in thought, to any one of them when we pray. For instance you can ask Bahá'u'lláh for something, or, thinking of Him, ask God for it. The same is true of the Master or the Guardian. You can turn in thought to either of them and then ask their intercession, or pray direct to God. As long as you don't confuse their stations, and make them all equal, it does not matter much how you orient your thoughts.[43]

What we should be very clear about, though, is that we are not praying *to* the Master or to the Guardian. We are praying, with their help, to God; we are asking for their intercession. Shoghi Effendi, in a most moving passage, written after the passing of the Greatest Holy Leaf, addressed her in meditation:

Then intercede thou for me before the throne of the Almighty, O thou who, within the Company on High, dost intercede for all of humankind.[44]

One is able to concentrate one's mind this way but also for private prayer we need conditions of quietness. 'Abdu'l-Bahá says,

Prayer verily bestoweth life, particularly when offered in

private and at times, such as midnight, when freed from daily care.[45]

This is surely wise: to find a time in the day when you know you won't be disturbed and 'put a ring round it'; don't let anything interrupt this time of prayer and meditation. Private prayer helps concentration and true remembrance of God:

The reason why privacy hath been enjoined in moments of devotion is this, that thou mayest give thy best attention to the remembrance of God, that thy heart may at all times be animated with His Spirit, and not be shut out as by a veil from thy Best Beloved. Let not thy tongue pay lip service in praise of God while thy heart be not attuned to the exalted Summit of Glory, and the Focal Point of communion. Thus if haply thou dost live in the Day of Resurrection, the mirror of thy heart will be set towards Him Who is the Day-Star of Truth; and no sooner will His light shine forth than the splendour thereof shall forthwith be reflected in thy heart. For He is the Source of all goodness, and unto Him revert all things. But if He appeareth while thou hast turned unto thyself in meditation, this shall not profit thee, unless thou shalt mention His Name by words He hath revealed. For in the forthcoming Revelation it is He Who is the Remembrance of God, whereas the devotions which thou art offering at present have been prescribed by the Point of the Bayán, while He Who will shine resplendent in the Day of Resurrection is the Revelation of the inner reality enshrined in the Point of the Bayán – a Revelation more potent, immeasurably more potent, than the one which hath preceded it.[46]

Of course, the Báb was talking about the future coming of Bahá'u'lláh but the Resurrection can take place in our hearts daily: 'Thy heart is My home; sanctify it for My descent.'[47] Chanting or saying prayers aloud also helps one's concentration but for Westerners this takes a bit of getting used to. Whatever we do, though, Shoghi

Effendi emphasises flexibility. He advises us to use the meditations given by Bahá'u'lláh but he goes on to say, 'the believers must be left free in these details and allowed to have personal latitude in finding their own level of communion with God'.[48] Clearly, prayer is something that grows from the simplest to the profoundest levels and to repeat Dom John Chapman, you must 'pray as you can'.

Degrees of prayer

Prayer even for material things is permitted.[49] Of course, the highest prayer is motivated by neither fear of hell nor hope of heaven.[50] All levels of prayer are permissible, but, says 'Abdu'l-Bahá, the highest prayers are for entrance to the Kingdom: 'Beseech . . . whatsoever thou desirest. But wert thou to heed my advice thou wouldst desire naught save entrance into the Abhá Kingdom . . .'[51] However, I feel sure we cannot sit in judgement on another's prayer. Only God can see the heart of the soul praying.

No doubt the highest prayer is love for God and His Will. For example, Bahá'u'lláh says, in the Long Obligatory Prayer, 'I have desired only what Thou didst desire and love only what Thou dost love'; and again, in that same prayer, Bahá'u'lláh puts these words into our mouths: 'Look not upon my hopes and my doings, nay rather look upon Thy will that hath encompassed the heavens and the earth.'[52] St. Augustine said, 'Love [God] and do what you like.'[53] The length of the prayer is irrelevant. 'Its prolongation', says the Báb, 'hath not been and is not beloved by God.'[54] Indeed, the Guardian confirms this in a letter to a believer who has been ill:

He is delighted to hear you are now fully recovered and again
active in your important work for the Cause. However, you
should not neglect your health, but consider it the means
which enables you to serve. It – the body – is like a horse which
carries the personality and spirit, and as such should be well
cared for so it can do its work! You should certainly safeguard
your nerves, and force yourself to take time, and not only for
prayer and meditation, but for real rest and relaxation. We
don't have to pray and meditate for hours in order to be
spiritual.[55]

'A short prayer pierceth heaven' was the way St.
Augustine put it. There are times when a cry from the
heart can be enough!

Meditation and contemplation

Let us turn aside now and look at what is called
'meditation'. That precious book entitled *Prayers and
Meditations* is a treasury of Bahá'u'lláh's Revelation. How
do we understand this term?

The word 'meditation' comes from a Greek root
meaning 'to think about'. The well-known story about
Sir Isaac Newton is illuminating on this point. He is said
to have been sitting alone in his garden; he saw an apple
drop from the tree and he fell into speculation on the
power of gravity. Now Bahá'u'lláh says that the deepest
meditations are but reflections of that which is created
within ourselves by the Revelations of God. Let us look at
this:

O Salmán! All that the sages and mystics have said or written
have never exceeded, nor can they ever hope to exceed, the
limitations to which man's finite mind hath been strictly
subjected. To whatever heights the mind of the most exalted of
men may soar, however great the depths which the detached

and understanding heart can penetrate, such mind and heart can never transcend that which is the creature of their own conceptions and the product of their own thoughts. The meditations of the profoundest thinker, the devotions of the holiest of saints, the highest expressions of praise from either human pen or tongue, are but a reflection of that which hath been created within themselves, through the revelation of the Lord, their God. Whoever pondereth this truth in his heart will readily admit that there are certain limits which no human being can possibly transgress. Every attempt which, from the beginning that hath no beginning, hath been made to visualize and know God is limited by the exigencies of His own creation – a creation which He, through the operation of His own Will and for the purposes of none other but His own Self, hath called into being. Immeasurably exalted is He above the strivings of human mind to grasp His Essence, or of human tongue to describe His mystery.[56]

During meditation we are speaking with our own spirits. 'Abdu'l-Bahá says that 'man . . . cannot both speak and meditate . . . you put certain questions to your spirit and the spirit answers':[57]

. . . if the faculty of meditation is bathed in the inner light and characterized with divine attributes, the results will be confirmed.

The meditative faculty is akin to the mirror; if you put it before earthly objects it will reflect them. Therefore if the spirit of man is contemplating earthly subjects he will be informed of these.

But if you turn the mirror of your spirits heavenwards, the heavenly constellations and the rays of the Sun of Reality will be reflected in your hearts, and the virtues of the Kingdom will be obtained.

Therefore let us keep this faculty rightly directed – turning it to the heavenly Sun and not to earthly objects – so that we may discover the secrets of the Kingdom, and comprehend the allegories of the Bible and the mysteries of the spirit.

May we indeed become mirrors reflecting the heavenly realities, and may we become so pure as to reflect the stars of heaven.[58]

In his meditation, Newton sat in his garden and saw with his own eyes the fall of an apple. He then abstracted himself from his surroundings: 'When the power of insight is being used the outward power of vision does not see.'[59] He started to meditate and we know the world-shattering results. It was an object outside himself that precipitated Newton's thought processes. Likewise our meditations, as Bahá'ís, are stimulated by an Object outside ourselves – the Manifestation of God. Our meditations are not just subjective wishful thinking. They are reflections created within ourselves by the Revelation of God. So when Evelyn Underhill defines meditation as 'thinking in the presence of God',[60] she is fairly near the mark. Clearly, the soul must turn to spiritual things in order to reflect them:

Bahá'u'lláh says there is a sign (from God) in every phenomenon: the sign of the intellect is contemplation and the sign of contemplation is silence, because it is impossible for a man to do two things at one time – he cannot both speak and meditate.

It is an axiomatic fact that while you meditate you are speaking with your own spirit. In that state of mind you put certain questions to your spirit and the spirit answers: the light breaks forth and the reality is revealed.

You cannot apply the name 'man' to any being void of this faculty of meditation; without it he would be a mere animal, lower than the beasts.

Through the faculty of meditation man attains to eternal life; through it he receives the breath of the Holy Spirit – the bestowal of the Spirit is given in reflection and meditation.

The spirit of man is itself informed and strengthened during meditation; through it affairs of which man knew nothing are unfolded before his view. Through it he receives Divine inspiration, through it he receives heavenly food.

Meditation is the key for opening the doors of mysteries. In that state man abstracts himself: in that state man withdraws himself from all outside objects; in that subjective mood he is immersed in the ocean of spiritual life and can unfold the secrets of things-in-themselves. To illustrate this, think of man as endowed with two kinds of sight; when the power of insight is being used the outward power of vision does not see.

This faculty of meditation frees man from the animal nature, discerns the reality of things, puts man in touch with God.[61]

'Abdu'l-Bahá points out, however, that if we meditate on earthly things, 'this faculty brings forth from the invisible plane the sciences and arts.' Also:

. . . Through the meditative faculty inventions are made possible, colossal undertakings are carried out; through it governments can run smoothly. Through this faculty man enters into the very Kingdom of God.[62]

Shoghi Effendi goes so far as to say that 'God can inspire into our minds things that we had no previous knowledge of, if He desires to do so'.[63]

At this point it might be useful to consider the difference between 'meditation' and 'contemplation'. The Christian mystic thinks of contemplation as being a state beyond meditation, where even thinking is subdued and one is literally in the presence of God Himself. A Bahá'í believes this is impossible, so what does contemplation mean in the Bahá'í Faith?

The subject is vast and profound and libraries have been written about it; but Bahá'u'lláh does constantly use symbolic terms about God's 'Presence', the 'Face of God', the 'Tongue of Grandeur', the 'All-Glorious Beloved', and so on. On the other hand, He reveals:

'Immeasurably exalted is He above the strivings of human mind to grasp His essence, or of human tongue to describe His mystery.'[64] Our minds in their strivings can reach no further than the Manifestation. During meditation about Bahá'u'lláh we may still use, mentally at least, words. During contemplation there is no need of them: a man feels near to God; that is enough. He is in the 'Valley of True Poverty and Absolute Nothingness'.[65] Bahá'u'lláh says of it, 'When the pen set to picturing this station/It broke in pieces and the page was torn.'[66]

The Guardian sees no reason why Bahá'ís shouldn't be taught to meditate but he warns us about allowing superstitions or foolish ideas creeping into it.

Asceticism

Asceticism is not allowed in the Bahá'í Faith. For example, in religious movements, asceticism has often been associated with severe physical, or sometimes solitary, disciplines. In the Bahá'í Faith there is a deep respect for the body as the servant of the Spirit. The Báb explains with great beauty:

As this physical frame is the throne of the inner temple, whatever occurs to the former is felt by the latter. In reality that which takes delight in joy or is saddened by pain is the inner temple of the body, not the body itself. Since this physical body is the throne whereon the inner temple is established, God hath ordained that the body be preserved to the extent possible, so that nothing that causeth repugnance may be experienced. The inner temple beholdeth its physical frame, which is its throne. Thus, if the latter is accorded respect, it is as if the former is the recipient. The converse is likewise true.

Therefore, it hath been ordained that the dead body should be treated with the utmost honour and respect.[67]

Shoghi Effendi's words, quoted earlier, apply this principle in a practical way: 'We don't have to pray and meditate for hours in order to be spiritual.'[68] The reference to the length of the prayer does not, of course, lay down any rule that it should not be long or that it must be short. The instruction is designed to prevent the person praying from overtaxing his strength. Brevity or length have no necessary relationship with holiness but only to the sincere desires of the one praying.

Prayer and the community

Now I want to look at prayer in the community. In our Faith, prayer has a universal dimension. The whole Order of Bahá'u'lláh is founded on the Word of God. The very constitution of the majestic Universal House of Justice begins with a prayer. A unique gift to us in this Dispensation is the treasury of prayers we can use together in groups. God has shown us how to speak to Him in His own divine Words. 'Abdu'l-Bahá has told us to 'engage in prayer', 'harmoniously attuned one to another', 'with the result that out of this coming together, unity and affection shall grow and flourish in the human heart'.[69] Our very Temples are situated at the heart of a cluster of buildings representing the whole of society. 'Abdu'l-Bahá has written,

The Máshriqu'l-Adhkar has important accessories, which are accounted of the basic foundations. These are, school for orphan children, hospital and dispensary for the poor, home for the incapacitated, college for higher scientific education, and hospice . . . When these institutions . . . are built, the doors will be opened to all the nations and religions. There will be absolutely no line of demarcation drawn. Its charities will be

dispensed irrespective of colour and race. Its gates will be flung
wide open to mankind; prejudice towards none, love for all.
The central building will be devoted to the purpose of prayer
and worship. Thus . . . religion will become harmonized with
science, and science will be the handmaid of religion, both
showering their material and spiritual gifts on all humanity.[70]

The whole Bahá'í world is linked together at a Nineteen
Day Feast. Prayer, like rain, promotes the growth of our
children and as 'Abdu'l-Bahá says,

These children are even as young plants, and teaching them the
prayers is as letting the rain pour down upon them, that they
may wax tender and fresh, and the soft breezes of the love of
God may blow over them, making them to tremble with joy.[71]

2

The Power of Prayer

The influence of prayer on one's own soul and upon the souls of others in the community

This brings up the question of the power of prayer. Of course we must be sure that we do not look upon what has just been said about children as a superstition. During the period when I was a Unitarian minister, I remember baptising a particular child. His mother never darkened the doors of the church but she had her child christened because she believed that, if children were christened, 'they came on better'.

Bahá'u'lláh talks of the tremendous power of prayer, especially if it is spoken aloud. Let us listen to a favourite passage of many Bahá'ís:

Intone, O My servant, the verses of God that have been received by thee, as intoned by them who have drawn nigh unto Him, that the sweetness of thy melody may kindle thine own soul, and attract the hearts of all men. Whoso reciteth, in the privacy of his chamber, the verses revealed by God, the scattering angels of the Almighty shall scatter abroad the fragrance of the words uttered by his mouth, and shall cause the heart of every righteous man to throb. Though he may, at first, remain unaware of its effect yet the virtue of the grace vouchsafed unto him must needs sooner or later exercise its influence upon his soul. Thus have the mysteries of the Revelation of God been decreed by virtue of the Will of Him Who is the Source of power and wisdom.[1]

It is so beautiful, we may overlook its challenge, especially for our teaching work. The Master also tells us: 'It is incumbent upon thee to turn to the Kingdom of God and to pray, supplicate and invoke during all times', because 'this is the means by which thy soul shall ascend upward to the apex of the gift of God'.[2] He also says,

Turn to God, supplicate humbly at His threshold, seeking assistance and confirmation, that God may rend asunder the veils that obscure your vision. Then will your eyes be filled with illumination, face to face you will behold the reality of God and your heart become completely purified from the dross of ignorance, reflecting the glories and bounties of the kingdom.[3]

Certain prayers have been endowed by Bahá'u'lláh with especial power. Shoghi Effendi wrote to an individual believer,

. . . the obligatory prayers are by their very nature of greater effectiveness and are endowed with a greater power than the non-obligatory ones . . .[4]

He also places the Tablet of Aḥmad and the Long Healing Prayer in this same category of powerful prayers.

The obligatory prayers

You often hear people say they don't like the idea of obligatory prayers and one may very well ask why there is this moral compulsion, as it were. Let us think about it. To begin with, I wonder how many of us would remember to pray if we were left entirely free in this

matter. 'Abdu'l-Bahá says that children must be 'continually reminded to remember their God'.[5] We are still
God's children and I believe we all need this reminder.
Neglect of our prayer-life leads to the withering of our
spiritual self, as St. Teresa says:

Even those who have reached great heights of prayer will find
it necessary, when from time to time God is pleased to prove
them and His Majesty seems to have forsaken them. For, as I
have already said – and I should not like this to be forgotten – in
this life of ours the soul does not grow in the way the body
does, though we speak as if it did, and growth does in fact
occur. But whereas a child, after attaining to the full stature of
a man, does not diminish in size so that his body becomes small
again, in spiritual matters the Lord is pleased that such
diminution should take place – at least, according to my own
observation, for I have no other means of knowing. This must
be in order to humble us for our greater good.[6]

Then there is the thought that by using this obligatory
prayer, we form a 'ring of prayer' all round the world all
the time. That fits in with the meaning of the Latin root of
'obligatory'. 'Obligatory' means 'imperative', 'morally
binding'; the Latin root 'ligare' means 'to bind' – and of
course, the word 'religion' stems from the same Latin
root and means 'to bind together'. This suggests the
thought that when we say our obligatory prayers, Bahá'ís
in every part of the world become linked together by
prayer. The prayers are morally binding upon each one of
us but also bind us together as a world community.

At this point I would like us to think about another
important aspect of our obligatory prayers, which is
expressed by 'Abdu'l-Bahá in the following two extracts:

The obligatory prayers are binding inasmuch as they are
conducive to humility and submissiveness, to setting one's

face towards God and expressing devotion to Him. Through such prayer man holdeth communion with God, seeketh to draw near unto Him, converseth with the true Beloved of one's heart, and attaineth spiritual stations.[7]

It behoveth the servant to pray to and seek assistance from God, and to supplicate and implore His aid. Such becometh the rank of servitude, and the Lord will decree whatsoever He desireth, in accordance with His consummate wisdom.[8]

Notice the element of training in obedience and humility here; the daily reminder of our relationship to God and His Manifestation: 'Such becometh the rank of servitude . . . ' Indeed, 'Abdu'l-Bahá speaks of the hidden wisdom of these prayers:

Know thou that in every word and movement of the obligatory prayer there are allusions, mysteries and a wisdom that man is unable to comprehend, and letters and scrolls cannot contain.[9]

The Guardian also talks about the special potency of regular recitation of the obligatory prayers:

You should rest assured that your strict adherence to the laws and observances enjoined by Bahá'u'lláh is the one power that can effectively guide and enable you to overcome the tests and trials of your life, and help you to continually grow and develop spiritually.

The Guardian particularly appreciates the fact that you have been faithfully observing Bahá'u'lláh's injunction regarding the recital of the daily obligatory prayers, and have thereby set such a high example before your Bahá'í fellow-youth. These daily prayers have been endowed with a special potency which only those who regularly recite them can adequately appreciate. The friends should therefore endeavour to make daily use of these prayers, whatever the peculiar circumstances and conditions of their life.[10]

Bearing in mind the special potency of these prayers on our own characters, just imagine their world-transforming effect if every Bahá'í obeys this Law of Bahá'u'lláh! He has been very kind to our frail humanity. The Short Obligatory Prayer is very short. It takes only a few minutes to say. We need to train ourselves in this daily habit. Nor do we *always* need to *understand* why we have to do certain things. The very act of obedience to Bahá'u'lláh, because we love His Will, brings us His grace and leads to our spiritual progress: 'For my yoke is easy, and my burden is light.'[11] Shoghi Effendi wrote to an individual believer these words:

He would advise you to only use the short midday Obligatory Prayer. This has no genuflections and only requires that when saying it the believer turn his face towards 'Akká where Bahá'u'lláh is buried. This is a physical symbol of an inner reality, just as the plant stretches out to the sunlight – from which it receives life and growth – so we turn our hearts to the Manifestation of God, Bahá'u'lláh, when we pray; and we turn our faces, during this short prayer, to where His dust lies on this earth as a symbol of the inner act.

Bahá'u'lláh has reduced all ritual and form to an absolute minimum in His Faith. The few forms that there are – like those associated with the two longer obligatory daily prayers, are only symbols of the inner attitude. There is a wisdom in them, and a great blessing, but we cannot force ourselves to understand or feel these things, that is why He gave us also the very short and simple prayer, for those who did not feel the desire to perform the acts associated with the other two.[12]

So you see, there is *ritual* in the Faith. According to the *Concise Oxford Dictionary*, a 'rite' is a 'form of procedure, an action required or usual in a religious or solemn ceremony'. We don't have to be afraid of a little ritual, as long as it means something. As the Faith develops there

may well be more given to us by the Universal House of
Justice out of their deductions from the Writings. There
are, for example, rituals connected with pilgrimage to the
Most Great House in Baghdad; but these belong to the
future and Shoghi Effendi has written: 'The simplicity
characterising the offering of Bahá'í prayers, whether
obligatory or otherwise, should be maintained. Rigidity
and rituals should be strictly avoided.'[13] It follows, then,
that what rituals there are in the Faith are designed to help
our spiritual growth. To quote again from the passage
cited above:

This is a physical symbol of an inner reality, just as the plant
stretches out to the sunlight – from which it receives life and
growth – so we turn our hearts to the Manifestation of God,[14]

Shoghi Effendi has also written through his secretary:

Concerning the directions given by Bahá'u'lláh for the recital
of certain prayers, Shoghi Effendi wishes me to inform you
that these regulations – which by the way are very few and
simple – are of a great spiritual help to the individual believer,
in that they help him to fully concentrate when praying and
meditating. Their significance is thus purely spiritual.[15]

Just as, in prayer, it is the inner meaning of the words that
matters, so with our ritual acts. We are expressing
meaningful attitudes with our bodies.

The meaning of the Qiblih, the Point of Adoration, to
which we turn in prayer, is perhaps the most important
ritual act of all. It concentrates all our attention on the
Manifestation of God by our turning to His earthly
resting-place. Shoghi Effendi cautions us, though. He
says:

In prayer the believers can turn their consciousness toward the
Shrine of Bahá'u'lláh, provided that in doing so they have a

clear and correct understanding of His station as a Manifestation of God.[16]

Prayers for one's parents are blessed

Turning now to a new subject, let us think about those prayers we are bidden to offer for the souls of those in the 'Abhá Kingdom – souls whose spiritual progress depends on prayer and the mercy of God. I suppose many Bahá'ís with a Protestant background find this concept difficult. When He was in London, 'Abdu'l-Bahá said,

Those who have ascended have different attributes from those who are still on earth, yet there is no real separation.

In prayer there is a mingling of station, a mingling of condition. Pray for them as they pray for you![17]

In a talk to Miss E. J. Rosenberg in 1904, 'Abdu'l-Bahá also explained:

The grace of effective intercession is one of the perfections belonging to advanced souls, as well as to the Manifestations of God. Jesus Christ had the power of interceding for the forgiveness of His enemies when on earth, and He certainly has this power now. 'Abdu'l-Bahá never mentions the name of a dead person without saying 'May God forgive him!' or words to that effect. Followers of the prophets have also this power of praying for the forgiveness of souls. Therefore we may not think that any souls are condemned to a stationary condition of suffering or loss arising from absolute ignorance of God. The power of effective intercession for them always exists . . .

The rich in the other world can help the poor, as the rich can help the poor here. In every world all are the creatures of God. They are always dependent on Him. They are not independent and can never be so. While they are needful of God, the more they supplicate, the richer they become. What is their merchandise, their wealth? In the other world what is help and assistance? It is intercession. Undeveloped souls must gain progress at first through the supplications of the spiritually rich; afterwards they can progress through their own supplications.[18]

Prayers for our parents are especially commanded. Indeed, the Báb advises us that after each prayer we should supplicate God 'to bestow mercy and forgiveness' upon our parents. Here are His Words:

It is seemly that the servant should, after each prayer, supplicate God to bestow mercy and forgiveness upon his parents. Thereupon God's call will be raised: 'Thousand upon thousand of what thou hast asked for thy parents shall be thy recompense!' Blessed is he who remembereth his parents when communing with God. There is, verily, no God but Him, the Mighty, the Well-Beloved.[19]

This privilege should surely comfort us as well as giving us the assurance that our service to the Cause rendered in our parents' names can help their progress in the next world. In the *Tablets of 'Abdu'l-Bahá* we come across these words of a prayer:

O Lord! In this Most Great Dispensation Thou dost accept the intercession of children in behalf of their parents. This is one of the special infinite bestowals of this Dispensation. Therefore, O Thou kind Lord, accept the request of this Thy servant at the threshold of Thy singleness and submerge his father in the ocean of Thy grace, because this son hath arisen to render Thee service and is exerting effort at all times in the pathway of Thy love.[20]

Thanksgiving is conducive to increase in bounty

This brings me to a very important aspect of prayer: that of thanksgiving. We tend to think of prayer as petition – a kind of spiritual shopping list. But besides petition there

are the prayers of adoration, thanksgiving, confession,
consecration and communion. 'Abdu'l-Bahá says, 'Be
thou happy and well pleased and arise to offer thanks to
God, in order that thanksgiving may conduce to increase
of bounty.'[21] Many of the prayers revealed for us begin
and end in notes of thanksgiving or adoration: we have
only to refer to our prayer book to see this. Day by day we
should likewise begin and end in God. Listen to 'Abdu'l-
Bahá's words:

Do you realize how much you should thank God for His
blessings? If you should thank Him a thousand times with each
breath it would not be sufficient, because God has created and
trained you. He has protected you from every affliction and
prepared every gift and bestowal. Consider what a kind Father
He is . . . He has given us a kind father and compassionate
mother, . . . refreshing water, gentle breezes and the sun
shining above our heads. In brief, He has supplied all the
necessities of life although we did not ask for any of these great
gifts . . .
    . . . You must appreciate the value of this bounty and
engage your time in mentioning and thanking the True One.[22]

3

Prayer and Action

Of course, praising God is not just a matter of shutting oneself in one's chamber and becoming abstracted in prayer. In the Bahá'í Faith, prayer is intimately related to action.

Recognition and obedience

Bahá'u'lláh says there is a two-fold obligation imposed upon us: to recognise Him and to obey His commands. He says that faith and deeds are both necessary; neither is acceptable without the other:

The first duty prescribed by God for His servants is the recognition of Him Who is the Day Spring of His Revelation and the Fountain of His laws, Who representeth the Godhead in both the Kingdom of His Cause and the world of creation. Whoso achieveth this duty hath attained unto all good; and whoso is deprived thereof, hath gone astray, though he be the author of every righteous deed. It behoveth every one who reacheth this most sublime station, this summit of transcendent glory, to observe every ordinance of Him Who is the Desire of the world. These twin duties are inseparable. Neither is acceptable without the other. Thus hath it been decreed by Him Who is the Source of Divine inspiration.[1]

That is challenging if you like and needs some serious thinking. One might describe it as a 'hard saying'! Bahá'u'lláh says quite clearly that good works are not enough: belief in Him is essential. Is there a difference, perhaps, between being 'acceptable' and being 'saved'? After all, man is body, mind and spirit. Christ used the same challenge as Bahá'u'lláh but with the opposite emphasis:

Not everyone who says to me, 'Lord, Lord', shall enter the kingdom of heaven, but he who does the will of my Father who is in heaven.[2]

He was clearly emphasising good works to those who laid too much stress on belief on its own. Perhaps Bahá'u'lláh, coming in the middle of the nineteenth century when good works were very much the order of the day, at least in the Christian Faith, was aware that belief (faith) would wane and so the reason for caring for one's fellow-men might become clouded. He is concerned with inner motivation.

Emerging from all this is the fact that prayer, plus obedience to divine Law, plus service, brings about transformation of character. Let us read some words of Shoghi Effendi:

He wishes again to assure you he will pray for your spiritual advancement in the Holy Shrines. The power of God can entirely transmute our characters and make of us beings entirely unlike our previous selves. Through prayer and supplication, obedience to the divine laws Bahá'u'lláh has revealed, and ever-increasing service to His Faith, we can change ourselves.[3]

The believers, as we all know, should endeavour to set such an example in their personal lives and conduct that others will feel impelled to embrace a Faith which reforms human character. However, unfortunately, not everyone achieves easily and rapidly the victory over self. What every believer, new or old, should realize is that the Cause *has* the spiritual power to re-create us if we make the effort to let that power influence us, and the greatest help in this respect is prayer. We must supplicate Bahá'u'lláh to assist us to overcome the failings in our own characters, and also exert our own will power in mastering ourselves.[4]

Prayer and meditation are very important factors in deepening the spiritual life of the individual, but with them must go also action and example, as these are the tangible results of the former. Both are essential.[5]

St. Paul told the early Christians at Corinth, 'I die daily.'[6] Day by day the ego was subdued. I think this is the crux of the matter: the potentially good Bahá'í is the one who is willing to change, to conform, gradually, to the Law of Bahá'u'lláh, out of love for Him. Yes, becoming a Bahá'í is a continuous process and we have to be patient with one another and with ourselves. Do you remember the time when Colby Ives despaired of reaching the standards 'Abdu'l-Bahá placed before him? He describes it in these words:

Under the influence of such tremendous thoughts as these I one day asked 'Abdu'l-Bahá how it could ever be possible for me, deep in the mass of weak and selfish humanity, ever to hope to attain when the goal was so high and great. He said that it is to be accomplished little by little; little by little. And I thought to myself, I have all eternity for this journey from self to God. The thing to do is to get started.[7]

Brother Lawrence said he felt the presence of God when he was working among his pots and pans in the monastery kitchen just as much as he did in the chapel;[8] but there is no doubt that this sense of the presence of God in his daily life was precisely because of what he did in the chapel. St. Teresa uses the symbolism of her age when she refers to the 'devil' but with her profound experience of prayer she makes the same point:

I can say what I know by experience – namely that no one who has begun this practice, however many sins he may commit, should ever forsake it. For it is the means by which we may amend our lives again, and without it amendment will be very much harder. So let him not be tempted by the devil, as I was, to give it up for reasons of humility.[9]

They will know, by the improvement which they discern in themselves, that this is not the work of the devil. For, even though they keep falling, there is one sign that the Lord has been with them – namely, the speed with which they rise again.[10]

We can never hope to feel the presence of God unless we do spend time with Him in our private times of prayer. There is a time, indeed, when action merges into prayer and prayer into action.

At the Dublin International Conference in 1982, the Hand of the Cause John Robarts spoke about the wonderful services of the late Hand of the Cause Dr. Adelbert Mühlschlegel. He had given his whole life in the service of the Cause but in his last years he still wished to serve, by pioneering to Athens. When he went there he was as 'frail as a feather and clear as a bell' but he was oppressed by the constraints of his physical weakness. He said, in effect, 'I have failed. I came here to teach the Bahá'ís and to deepen them.' But the truth was far otherwise. The fact that Dr. Mühlschlegel was there, in Athens, at his age; that except for his wife he was alone there after a lifetime's sacrificial service, was a shining example more potent than any words. In him action and prayer had become one in a radiant heart that shed light and guidance on all around him.

Prayer and the World Order of Bahá'u'lláh

If we look for a wider expression of prayer in action we can do no better than turn to the Bahá'í community world-wide. Surely this is the practical result of the Holy Words and prayers of Bahá'u'lláh! And world peace, which all peoples on the earth long for, cannot ultimately be established without Bahá'u'lláh's World Order. This Order is the divine foundation of a new world; and you and I are involved in building it. It is wonderful how Bahá'u'lláh mingles the spiritual law for the individual and for the planet. He expresses it perfectly and so simply, in the *Hidden Words*:

O Children of Men! Know ye not why We created you all from the same dust? That no one should exalt himself over the other. Ponder at all times in your hearts how ye were created. Since We have created you all from one same substance it is incumbent on you to be even as one soul, to walk with the same feet, eat with the same mouth and dwell in the same land, that from your inmost being, by your deeds and actions, the signs of oneness and the essence of detachment may be made manifest. Such is My counsel to you, O concourse of light! Heed ye this counsel that ye may obtain the fruit of holiness from the tree of wondrous glory.[11]

Each one of us has the privilege of drawing strength from this universal Faith of ours and of giving our strength to its service. We can walk the mystical path with practical feet. We can pray and teach and keep always the idea of 'delivering the Message' at the forefront of our minds. We should never lose an opportunity of mentioning the

Faith, whether it be to a person we meet, or in our letters, or over the telephone. We should never miss an opportunity of being kind to our neighbours, of helping anyone we meet casually, where there is a need.

Constant prayer, as an expression of our love for Bahá'u'lláh, is the life-line linking us to that Power and Guidance that will make our daily efforts possible. And we are not alone. When a man falls in love with Bahá'u'lláh he enters into a new society, a new environment. Within this new environment powerful spiritual forces are flowing. Its heart is beating at the World Centre; from it the pulsating life of the Cause is flowing through the national and local assemblies, manifesting its spiritual energies within Nineteen Day Feasts and individual believers and returning to the heart of the Cause. Under the guidance of the Universal House of Justice, Hands of the Cause, Counsellors, Auxiliary Board Members and their Assistants bring direction and inspiration to this World Order. Very severe tests come to us all but if we all obey the Law of Bahá'u'lláh we are surrounded by a beloved community, by an Order through whose body pulsates a healing life. If, by the grace of Bahá'u'lláh, we face our tests with courage, they can become a source of blessing, making us stronger, a little more mature and grown up to face life. As the Guardian wrote:

One thing and only one thing will unfailingly and alone secure the undoubted triumph of this sacred Cause, namely, the extent to which our own inner life and private character mirror forth in their manifold aspects the splendour of those eternal principles proclaimed by Bahá'u'lláh.[12]

PART II

Prayer as a Living Reality

by
Madeline Hellaby

I

God as a Friend

I fled Him, down the nights and down the days;
  I fled Him, down the arches of the years;
I fled Him, down the labyrinthine ways
  Of my own mind; and in the mist of tears
I hid from Him, and under running laughter.
      Up vistaed hopes I sped;
      And shot, precipitated,
Adown Titanic glooms of chasmèd fears,
  From those strong Feet that followed, followed
      after.
      But with unhurrying chase,
      And unperturbèd pace,
  Deliberate speed, majestic instancy,
      They beat – and a Voice beat
      More instant than the Feet –
  'All things betray thee, who betrayest Me.'

The poet then describes his efforts to flee and find solace
in other things; then, at the end, he says,

      Now of that long pursuit
      Comes on at hand the bruit;
  That Voice is round me like a bursting sea:
      'And is thy earth so marred,
      Shattered in shard on shard?
  Lo, all things fly thee, for thou fliest Me!
      Strange, piteous, futile thing!

Wherefore should any set thee love apart?
Seeing none but I makes much of naught' (He
    said),
'And human love needs human meriting:
    How hast thou merited –
Of all man's clotted clay the dingiest clot?
    Alack, thou knowest not
How little worthy of any love thou art!
Whom wilt thou find to love ignoble thee,
    Save Me, save only Me?
All which I took from thee I did but take,
    Not for thy harms,
But just that thou might'st seek it in My
    arms.
    All which thy child's mistake
Fancies as lost, I have stored for thee at home:
    Rise, clasp My hand, and come!'
    Halts by me that footfall:
    Is my gloom, after all,
Shade of His hand, outstretched caressingly?
    'Ah, fondest, blindest, weakest,
    I am He Whom thou seekest!
Thou dravest love from thee, who dravest
    Me.'

In this poem, *The Hound of Heaven*, one of the most brilliant ever written on the subject, Francis Thompson describes vividly his attempt to run away from God. Like all created things, he wanders 'distracted in search of the Friend';[1] but as St. Augustine said, 'Thou hast made us for Thyself and our hearts are restless till they find rest in Thee.'[2] Francis Thompson was, in fact, searching for the Friend, although to begin with he did not realise this. God knew His love for us, therefore He created us, has engraved His image on us and revealed His beauty to us; so naturally, there is an hunger in our souls: a desire to find the Giver of such tremendous gifts, even if, initially, we look in the wrong places. Once the Friend has been found and His love tested, then we can agree with Polonius, who, amongst other things in his famous speech to his son Laertes, told him,

> Those friends thou hast, and their adoption tried,
> Grapple them to thy soul with hoops of steel.[3]

We are God's friends. Bahá'u'lláh, in the *Hidden Words*, addresses us as such: 'O My friends!' 'O My friend!' He also frequently describes God as our Friend, our True Friend.

We all want a 'best friend' – one with whom we feel entirely at ease and with whom we share the most intimate thoughts of our hearts; one with whom we share common interests, aspirations, experiences, joys and sorrows; one who we know will love us whatever we may say or do and who will overlook our faults because he loves us. We need this kind of human friendship: how much more a spiritual one!

How do we become friends with God? Bahá'u'lláh tells us that He is transcendent. In order to become friends with someone, you have to get to know him; and to get to know someone, you have to meet and be introduced. How do we get to know God? How do we meet Him?

Well, for most of us, someone has already made the necessary introduction – usually our parents in the first instance. But this introduction is not necessarily a terribly adequate one and we may need another in later life: a friend, a book, a chance comment or a challenging question, a kind action which we experience or witness, suffering heroically borne. Whatever it is, it has made us think and become aware that our restlessness and unsatisfied desires are not caused, as we thought, by unsympathetic parents, an uncongenial job or any of the other excuses with which we deceive ourselves, but *spiritual* hunger which craves satisfaction and which will keep us in a continual state of tension and unhappiness until we listen to it and *do* something about it.

Having met God, we can now concentrate on getting to know Him. There are many ways of doing this but one of the best – and the one we are concerned with here – is through prayer; but that relationship may well echo, in our prayer life, the struggle that Francis Thompson describes in his outward search for God.

Personal friendships are the most transforming influences in our lives; so friendship with God will change the quality and tone of our life. He is closer to us than our life-vein.[4] If our life-vein is necessary for our physical life and He is closer than that, then He is telling us that our spiritual life is more important than our physical life. Indeed, we know it is, for this is the life which continues into the Abhá Kingdom. No wonder our Friend wants to help us!

2

Lord, Teach us how to Pray

Some two thousand years ago the disciples had to ask Christ to teach them how to pray – and we are still asking. A simple start is, of course, to use the prayers of the Manifestation of God. Christ left only one, the 'Lord's Prayer', which one might describe as the obligatory prayer of the Christian dispensation. Bahá'u'lláh has left a couple of hundred (probably more, as yet untranslated), including three obligatory prayers. But whether only one or a bookful, if you study them, you will learn a lot about praying.

The first thing you will notice, as was said earlier, is that they begin and end in God and the requests come in the middle. A study of their content is also invaluable in learning something about the spiritual life.

Another important point is that, in order to become proficient in anything, one must practise. This depends on three things: self-discipline, regularity and perseverance. We will consider them on two levels, the practical and the spiritual.

Practical

We have already dealt, earlier, with the need for a focus

for one's attention while praying, so there is no need to say any more on this matter, except to repeat how important it is that we have one.

Self-discipline is very necessary when one is, say, learning to play the piano. Unless one concentrates and controls one's fingers, one will never learn the piece and be able to play it properly. It is also necessary to *make* oneself practise, even if one doesn't always feel like it. One can play oneself into the mood.

The pianist knows that the regularity of his practising is vitally important and that without it, daily, his performance suffers. A famous musician – though nobody seems to know for certain who – said that if he missed one day's practice, *he* noticed the difference, if he missed two days, his family noticed the difference and if he missed three days, the public noticed it.

If you have ever heard a real musician doing his practice, you will know that he will work at the same little difficult passage, playing it over and over again until he has mastered it and he can play the piece through without stumbling any more at that same hurdle; and if, sometimes, he has a 'bad day', he will persevere regardless. He does not let these minor upsets deflect him from his purpose. When, finally, he has mastered the notes, he then sets about getting it learnt – and the true musician will learn it by heart as distinct from merely committing it to memory. It's worth all it costs.

The practice of the presence of God also requires self-discipline, regularity and perseverance. We are in the process of acquiring a habit, a good habit: the life of prayer; and we are in the process of becoming proficient at it.

Spiritual

We may need to *make* ourselves go and pray to begin with, but when we realise the importance of it we will soon be able to pray ourselves into the mood and to concentrate our minds. If our thoughts wander, as they frequently do, at least to begin with, we should not get worked up and feel guilty about it, for this merely uses up valuable energy in worrying which could be better employed in praying. No, we should just go gently after our thoughts and bring them back; and I am sure that God, one of Whose names is the Humorist, must constantly be amused at the stray thoughts about the dinner or the income tax forms that rise up to Him in the middle of our prayers!

Because, like unwilling children not wanting to leave their play in order to practise, we do not take to praying by instinct, God has ensured that we at least do the minimum in remembering Him by giving us, in the obligatory prayers, some specific times for praying. Our ordinary daily lives are so full that we all echo the words of one of Cromwell's officers, Sir Jacob Astley, before one of the battles of the Civil War (and with considerably less excuse): 'Lord, I shall be busy today. If I forget Thee, do Thou not forget me.' 'Abdu'l-Bahá says,

Supplication to God at morn and eve is conducive to the joy of hearts, and prayer causes spirituality and fragrance. Thou shouldst necessarily continue therein.[1]

We know also that we should commune with God at the dawn of every day and we should not lay our head on our pillow at the end of the day without saying our evening prayers. Once these obligations become part of our consciousness we cannot imagine ourselves ever not fulfilling them. The regularity of our spiritual meals becomes as vital to us as our physical ones – and note that the word 'vital' comes from the Latin word for 'life'. When we achieve this degree of consciousness in our spiritual life, if we miss one day's praying, *we* shall notice the difference, if we miss two days, our family will notice the difference, and if we miss three days, well, without doubt the public will notice that too.

As with anything worth doing, we have to persevere if we are ever to become proficient at it. We need to grow beyond the idea that unless we really *feel* the presence of God when we pray, we are not really praying. What the Christian mystics call 'consolations' are not everyday occurrences and we should certainly not give up trying because our prayers appear to be 'dry'. We should not even seek these experiences but persevere in our praying, leaving it to God to use our prayers as He sees fit and not wanting any superficial and temporary benefit to ourselves.

Forming a habit, therefore, depends on self-discipline, regularity and perseverance. These, in turn, depend on motivation; motivation depends on conviction; conviction depends on faith; faith depends on love; love depends on knowledge – so we are back where we started: meeting, getting to know and loving God.

Praying is fundamentally a matter of expressing our love for God. Learning to pray, too, is worth all it costs. Even so, we may feel that our prayers aren't worth much. The practice of the presence of God is all right in theory but in practice we may utterly fail to feel this presence. We shall deal with this in the next chapter.

3

The Practice of the Presence of God

The practice of the presence of God is far from simple. There are several things on which it depends:

Character

If God seems unreal to us, perhaps the first thing we should do is follow Fosdick's advice:

> . . . he may well search his life for sinister habits of thought, for cherished evils dimly recognised as wrong but unsurrendered, for lax carelessness in conduct or deliberate infidelity to conscience, for sins whose commission he deplores, but whose results he still clings to and desires, and above all for selfishness that hinders loving and so breaks the connections that bind us to God and one another.[1]

Purity of heart

'Be pure, be pure!' cries Bahá'u'lláh. 'The time is come', the Báb told the Letters of the Living, 'when naught but the purest motive, supported by deeds of stainless purity, can ascend unto the throne of the Most High and be acceptable unto Him.'[2] How often do we have a motive which is one hundred percent pure? Perhaps here we have a potent reason for ineffectiveness in praying. Certainly, unless we do come to our prayers with a pure heart, we have no hope at all of drawing anywhere near to the door of His gate, let alone the throne of the Most High.

Vindictiveness

God can never seem real to us if we try to approach Him with thorns of hate or thistles of malice towards another in our hearts. Christ told His followers *exactly* what to do:

Therefore if thou bring thy gift to the altar, and there rememberest that thy brother hath ought against thee;
Leave there thy gift before the altar, and go thy way; first be reconciled to thy brother, and then come and offer thy gift.[3]

Not an easy thing to do. It requires that we humble ourselves before our brother; but we shall never be right with God until we are right with the one to whom we have done wrong, or even if we feel we are the injured party. We shall not find Him if we retain one single trace of malice or mischief in our heart towards someone else, especially towards one who has done nothing more than irritate us.

Moods

Certain things in life one has to do whether one feels like it or not: one has to go to work, get meals ready, attend to the children and so on. A person who gives way to variable moods will not be efficient: he will not achieve much. The same attitude is necessary in a life of prayer. One has to work at it. We saw earlier how Brother Lawrence said he felt the presence of God as much in his kitchen, working amongst his pots and pans, as he did in the chapel; but that it was precisely *because* of what went on in the chapel – the regular feeding of his soul in prayer – that he was able to feel the presence of God amongst the ordinary mundane duties of his day. In these early days of the Faith, most of us do not even have a House of Worship to aid our devotions, we have to offer them in the individual privacy of our own homes; but if we do this regularly and faithfully, there is no reason why the result should not be the same. It is harder, perhaps, but there is all the more merit in that!

One also has to remember that the heights of fellowship with God are not often reached. The Mount of Transfiguration is a genuine experience in prayer but it does not come very often and certainly not for the asking. As the hymn-writer says:

> Not always on the mount may we
> Rapt in the heavenly vision be;
> The shores of thought and feeling know
> The Spirit's tidal ebb and flow.
>
> 'Lord, it is good abiding here,'
> We cry, the heavenly presence near:
> The vision vanishes, our eyes
> Are lifted into vacant skies.
>
> Yet hath one such exalted hour
> Upon the soul redeeming power,
> And in its strength through after days
> We travel our appointed ways;
>
> Till all the lowly vale grows bright,
> Transfigured in remembered light,
> And in untiring souls we bear
> The freshness of the upper air.
>
> The mount of vision: but below
> The paths of daily duty go,
> And nobler life therein shall own
> The pattern on the mountain shown.[4]

Probably far more often our prayer-times are commonplace (the vacant skies) and we must be patient with them. Sometimes, indeed, it seems as if God has withdrawn altogether and then we experience a real 'dark night of the soul', as St. John of the Cross calls it.[5] At these times, phrases in Bahá'u'lláh's prayers such as 'Thou beholdest me, O my God, clinging to the cord of Thy mercy' spring to life; for it may be that we have nothing else to cling on to in our life, at that moment, and if that cord snapped . . . but we know it never will! Sooner or later the clouds will disperse and we shall feel that presence again. It is as though God were saying to us: 'I must test your faith. You say you believe in Me, so let's see if you really mean it. I am going away for a little while. Will you still be there when I come back?' He hasn't really disappeared, of course; He has merely gone out of our immediate line of vision. He is really only hiding behind us, all the time!

Temperament

Some people seem to be spiritual geniuses and for them, we say, it's all right; but what of us who are not so gifted? We experience only a vague groping after God and often we seem only to be talking to the air. How can *we* practise the presence of God?

The best in us is God working through us, so although we may not have a gift for prayer as we may not have a gift for playing the piano, that does not cut us off from God any more than not being able to play divinely cuts us off from music. We need to look within:

Turn thy sight unto thyself, that thou mayest find Me standing within thee, mighty, powerful and self-subsisting![6]

If we want something badly enough, we don't just sit there twiddling our thumbs and waiting for it to happen; we get up and *do* something about it. If we want a good show of annuals in our garden, we don't just wait for the seeds to blow in from our neighbours' gardens, we go and buy a packet and plant them ourselves.

Also, have you ever stood by a rocky sea-shore when the tide is coming in, watching its flow inwards? It may flow unimpeded up the beach but it finds it hard to get through the narrow channels between the rocks. Standing there watching it, you can see that the vast ocean is behind it, whereas if you were lying on the beach you would see only the struggle. The water comes from the ocean, not from the rocks; and God made the rocks and narrow channels as well as the open strand. So He tries, through our best, to find even a narrow channel for His spirit to flow through.

Could it be that we try too hard to seek God? God is seeking *us* and His search precedes ours for Him. Sometimes we need to cease our frenzied search, relax and consent simply to be *found*: 'Be *still* and *know* that I am God'[7] (italics mine).

I particularly like Bahá'u'lláh's reply to someone who was obviously asking Him about the progress of the soul, perhaps saying that he thought he must be a pretty poor specimen because he had not gone through all the various grades of spiritual experience:

Much hath been written in the books of old concerning the various stages in the development of the soul, such as concupiscence, irascibility, inspiration, benevolence, content-ment, Divine good-pleasure, and the like; the Pen of the Most High, however, is disinclined to dwell upon them. Every soul that walketh humbly with its God, in this Day, and cleaveth unto Him, shall find itself invested with the honour and glory of all goodly names and stations.[8]

Thus Bahá'u'lláh reassured this seeking soul, making him realise that, though he might not be a spiritual genius, he could be just as great a recipient of God's bounty as anyone else.

4

Co-operation with God

'God can afford to dispense with all creatures'[1] has to be understood in its true context. Of course He can, in one sense: if *one* is lost there is always another and if *one* refuses to work for Him, He can raise up others who will.

It does not mean that God does not *need* man, because it is clear that He does. Bahá'u'lláh says that man's unique capacity 'to know Him and to love Him' 'must needs be regarded as the generating impulse and the primary purpose underlying the whole of creation'.[2] He talks about '. . . the destiny of the true believer, whose existence and life are to be regarded as the originating purpose of all creation'[3] and in Prayer No. 8 in *Bahá'í Prayers* He says, 'Thou didst wish to make Thyself known unto men; therefore Thou didst, through a word of Thy mouth, bring *creation* into being and fashion the *universe*' (italics mine). 'Abdu'l-Bahá tells us: 'If man did not exist, the universe would be without result, for the object of existence is the appearance of the perfections of God.'[4] The appearance of the perfections of God, which the Master has been talking about in that chapter, are very much the concern of the life of prayer.

One of the commonest fallacies about prayer is that God can do all He wishes without any help from us; but

Bahá'u'lláh says: 'Arise to aid thy Lord at all times and in all circumstances, and be thou one of His *helpers*'[5] (italics mine); and again, 'O friends! *Help* ye the one true God'[6] (italics mine). Notice that He calls us His friends once more – and you don't ask your friends for help unless you need it.

Two ways of helping

We can *think* – use our brains – employ that rational faculty which is man's distinguishing spirit. 'Abdu'l-Bahá tells us how the ability to think has enabled us to conquer nature and control her forces for our own use. Thought precedes any enterprise. God does not do our thinking for us.

We can *work*. God filled the Italian hills with marble but He did not build the Shrine of the Báb nor the seat of the Universal House of Justice!

Some things are contingent on praying

If some things which God wants done are contingent on thinking and working, why should not some be contingent on praying? It may be that for some things which God wants done, prayer is the only means available for doing them.

Resignation is not the only attitude in prayer. We are not resigned anywhere else. If we see oppression and injustice we don't just sit back and say, 'Oh, it is the will of God; we must be resigned to it.' We set about improving conditions, or whatever else needs doing. When Bahá'u'lláh says, 'O Children of Men! Know ye not why We created you all from the same dust? That no one should exalt himself over the other'[7] and ' . . . it is incumbent on you to be even as one soul, to walk with the same feet, eat with the same mouth and dwell in the same land',[8] we know without any shadow of doubt that this is what God wants; so we set about implementing this; and we shall not rest until we have finally established His Kingdom on earth. Our unresigned attitude is therefore seen, not as rebellion against God but co-operation *with* Him. Not 'Thy will be changed' but 'Thy will be done'! Where we are certain beyond all doubt that something is God's will – as, for instance, where we read in the Scriptures that 'It is Our will and desire that . . . ' or 'We love to see you at all times . . . ' then we can pray with complete confidence for the achievement of that purpose; and as we said, there are some areas where prayer is the only activity we *can* engage in. The most obvious example of this is in connection with Covenant-breakers. We have to shun them physically but there is no reason at all why we should not pray for them.

Listen, don't talk

We must learn to listen to God as well as to talk to Him. Madame de Staël, after a two hours' visit in which she talked all the time, is said to have remarked at parting, 'What a delightful conversation we have had!'[9] So many of our prayers are like that; but a conversation is a two-way process. In ordinary life, if we do all the talking, the other person is liable to go to sleep. Well, maybe God won't go to sleep – for we know He never does – but we are not likely to derive much benefit from our prayers if we never give Him a chance to say anything. We ring the front door bell but because the Master of the house is a long time coming, we become impatient and do not wait for an answer. In extreme cases, because He doesn't immediately respond to our ringing, we presume he doesn't live there any more and decide not to try in future.

Admittedly, *listening* to God may not be an easy state to get into, because it isn't a simple matter of hearing a voice. 'Abdu'l-Bahá has given us guidance. We have to learn the right language:

We should speak in the language of heaven – in the language of the spirit – for there is a language of the spirit and heart. It is as different from our language as our own language is different from that of the animals, who express themselves only by cries and sounds.

It is the language of the spirit which speaks to God. When, in prayer, we are freed from all outward things and turn to God, then it is as if in our hearts we hear the voice of God. Without words we speak, we communicate, we converse with God and hear the answer . . . All of us, when we attain to a truly spiritual condition, can hear the Voice of God.[10]

Giving is not a simple matter

Giving is not a simple matter either. It is a dual transaction. You may want to give somebody something but if that person in unwilling, or not ready, to receive your gift, then you cannot give it. In its supreme form, this unwillingness and unreadiness is expressed by Bahá'u'lláh, in the agony of His soul, when He says:

Oh, would that the world could believe Me! Were all the things that lie enshrined within the heart of Bahá, and which the Lord, His God, the Lord of all names, hath taught Him, to be unveiled to mankind, every man on earth would be dumbfounded.

How great the multitude of truths which the garment of

words can never contain! How vast the number of such verities as no expression can adequately describe, whose significance can never be unfolded, and to which not even the remotest allusions can be made! How manifold are the truths which must remain unuttered until the appointed time is come! Even as it hath been said: 'Not everything that a man knoweth can be disclosed, nor can everything that he can disclose be regarded as timely, nor can every timely utterance be considered as suited to the capacity of those who hear it.'

Of these truths some can be disclosed only to the extent of the capacity of the repositories of the light of Our knowledge, and the recipients of Our hidden grace. We beseech God to strengthen thee with His power, and enable thee to recognize Him Who is the Source of all knowledge, that thou mayest detach thyself from all human learning, for, 'what would it profit any man to strive after learning when he hath already found and recognized Him Who is the Object of all knowledge?' Cleave to the Root of Knowledge, and to Him Who is the Fountain thereof, that thou mayest find thyself independent of all who claim to be well versed in human learning, and whose claim no clear proof, nor the testimony of any enlightening book, can support.[11]

5

Prayer and the Reign of Law

Miracles

Miracles are the fulfilment of a higher law than we know. We think of them as 'interfering' with the laws of nature, of breaking the 'natural law'; but what is natural law? The dictionary[1] defines it as, in one sense, merely 'a law of nature' (the other sense does not concern us here). Fosdick calls it 'man's statement of how things regularly happen, so far as he has been able to observe them'.[2] But man has not, so far, catalogued the spiritual laws and therefore he is surprised when so-called 'miracles' happen. Miracles, to God, are as natural as sunrise.[3] All that happens is that a higher law than the one we thought immutable has come into play. We see this happening all the time:

Man alone has freedom, and, by his understanding or intellect, has been able to gain control of and adapt some of those natural laws to his own needs. By the power of his intellect he has discovered means by which he not only traverses great continents in express trains and crosses vast oceans in ships, but, like the fish he travels under water in submarines, and, imitating the birds, he flies through the air in airships.

Man has succeeded in using electricity in several ways – for light, for motive power, for sending messages from one end of the earth to the other – and by electricity he can even hear a voice many miles away!

By this gift of understanding or intellect he has also been able to use the rays of the sun to picture people and things, and even to capture the form of distant heavenly bodies.

We perceive in what numerous ways man has been able to bend the powers of nature to his will.[4]

If *we* are free to overcome one law with another on the same plane, God is surely able to overcome a law on the physical plane – which, after all, He has Himself made – with one on a higher, spiritual plane. We should not be surprised, therefore, when occasionally He does.

Scientific knowledge

Scientific knowledge makes some people give up God and not progress in knowledge of Him. I think this happens where they retain childish and undeveloped conceptions of God and these have proved inadequate. If you question somebody who says he doesn't believe in God, you will probably find that you don't believe in the God he doesn't believe in, either. In the West it is not so common, perhaps, to find crudely anthropomorphic conceptions of God as it may be amongst 'primitive' peoples, but western conceptions *are* coloured by the paintings of the great masters; and modern man rejects these.

Another reason for disbelief in God is that those who profess this have no understanding of the purpose of tests and so relinquish what belief they have as soon as they have a test for which they do not see the need: 'How could a loving God do this to me?' they cry, quite forgetting that, in their childhood, a loving parent often refused to fulfil their wishes and sometimes made them accept situations they didn't want to accept. Later, they were grateful for these disciplines. They did not cease to acknowledge and love their parents because of these things – and are we not all the children of God?

On both these aspects of the matter, Bahá'ís have teachings which can help such people. Indeed, there is a vast ocean of help in the Writings – so great that it would be impossible to do justice to it here; a whole chapter could be taken up with references!

God's providence

However, belief in God's providence ('The Lord will provide'), though perfectly justified and frequently experienced, must not be confused with an arrogant assumption that that providence must be exercised as we wish, whether in praying for rain when overall it would be better for more people to have it remain dry, or in attempts to deflect God from His purpose in our lives, or in our dealings with other people. Bahá'u'lláh made it abundantly clear Who was in charge in His Tablet to the Minister of the Sháh in Constantinople:

Dost thou believe thou hast the power to frustrate His Will, to hinder Him from executing His judgment, or to deter Him from exercising His sovereignty? Pretendest thou that aught in the heavens or in the earth can resist His Faith? No, by Him Who is the Eternal Truth! Nothing whatsoever in the whole of creation can thwart His Purpose. Cast away, therefore, the mere conceit thou dost follow, for mere conceit can never take the place of truth. Be thou of them that have truly repented and returned to God, the God Who hath created thee, Who hath nourished thee, and made thee a minister among them that profess thy faith.

Know thou, moreover, that He it is Who hath, by His own behest, created all that is in the heavens and all that is on the earth. How can, then, the thing that hath been created at His bidding prevail against Him?[5]

H. M. Stanley, the famous explorer, describing what prayer meant in his life, wrote:

Prayer made me stronger, morally and mentally, than any of my non-praying companions. It did not blind my eyes, or dull my mind, or close my ears; but, on the contrary, it gave me confidence. It did more; it gave me joy and pride in my work . . .[6]

Natural law

So natural law is not what superficial thinking makes it appear to be: water *can* be made to flow uphill; inanimate objects – and huge ones at that – *can* be made to fly. Even bigger ones, much heavier than water, can be made to float. We cannot *alter* natural laws, which, left to themselves, do function in an immutable fashion; but we can overcome the law of gravity by bringing into play a stronger law involving pumping or movement or the floating propensities of hollow objects. We can turn these natural laws to our advantage, as we have seen in the passage from *Paris Talks* already quoted. We are the masters and not the slaves of law-abiding forces. Nature can be used as well as obeyed.[7]

Cause and effect

Let us look for a moment at the law of cause and effect. There are two kinds of cause. Fosdick gives the following examples:

Atmospheric pressure making the wind blow is one sort.

A man sailing by that wind, skilfully tacking until he reaches his destination, is another sort.

Snow on the footpath may be removed by *natural* causes – sunshine and rain; or by *personal* causes – you may take a shovel and clear the path.[8]

So: law-abiding forces can be made the servants of personal will.

God's freedom

God does not violate any of His laws to answer prayer. He is not less free than we are. If we can bring stronger laws into play to overcome natural laws, so can He. He has not just made a machine and left it to run, only able to do anything with it by intervention. Providence *is* possible; but it may be that this conception is linked to the idea of, shall we say, the 'Most Great Plan' of God and the smaller plans He has ordained for any particular planet through its Manifestation.[9] The Most Great Plan is obviously totally beyond our finite minds to conceive but it must surely embrace not only natural law but also the higher, spiritual laws which we mentioned earlier.

Some prayers God must not answer

Some prayers God must not answer: He must not substitute our wish for His Plan:

Say: He ordaineth as He pleaseth, by virtue of His sovereignty, and doeth whatsoever He willeth at His own behest. He shall not be asked of the things it pleaseth Him to ordain. He, in truth, is the Unrestrained, the All-Powerful, the All-Wise.[10]

We can pray about everything but we must leave it to God to decide what is best. We only see a tiny fraction of the situation; He sees the whole of it:

O thou who art turning thy face towards God! Close thine eyes to all things else, and open them to the realm of the All-Glorious. Ask whatsoever thou wishest of Him alone; seek whatsoever thou seekest from Him alone. With a look He granteth a hundred thousand hopes, with a glance He healeth a hundred thousand incurable ills, with a glimpse He layeth balm on every wound, with a nod He freeth the hearts from the shackles of grief. He doeth as He doeth, and what recourse have we? He carrieth out His Will, He ordaineth what He pleaseth. Then better for thee to bow down thy head in submission, and put thy trust in the All-Merciful Lord.[11]

We may say we have 'faith in prayer' – and indeed, we may rightly have this faith as long as it doesn't imply that it is presumptuous and clamorous. Perhaps we could turn the phrase and say we prefer to talk about 'prayer in faith'; for although we may, as the Master says, ask whatever we wish of God, *this* prayer always ends with 'Thy will, not mine, be done'.

All things work together for good

St. Paul says, 'All things work together for good to them that love God'[12] and we must learn to believe and know this to be true. It is not a theory to be learned in order to pass exams and be forgotten afterwards. We do pass exams with it, of course – spiritual exams – but if we are wise, far from forgetting it afterwards, we shall cling on to it with increase in faith, for has not Bahá'u'lláh Himself stated,

I swear by My life! Nothing save that which profiteth them can befall My loved ones. To this testifieth the Pen of God, the Most Powerful, the All-Glorious, the Best-Beloved.[13]

He could hardly have put it more strongly! He also says:

Blessed is the man that hath acknowledged his belief in God and in His signs, and recognized that 'He shall not be asked of His doings'. Such a recognition hath been made by God the ornament of every belief, and its very foundation. Upon it must depend the acceptance of every goodly deed. Fasten your eyes upon it, that haply the whisperings of the rebellious may not cause you to slip.

Were He to decree as lawful the thing which from time immemorial had been forbidden, and forbid that which had, at all times, been regarded as lawful, to none is given the right to question His authority. Whoso will hesitate, though it be for less than a moment, should be regarded as a transgressor.

Whoso hath not recognized this sublime and fundamental verity, and hath failed to attain this most exalted station, the winds of doubt will agitate him, and the sayings of the infidels will distract his soul. He that hath acknowledged this principle will be endowed with the most perfect constancy. All honour to this all-glorious station, the remembrance of which adorneth every exalted Tablet. Such is the teaching which God bestoweth on you, a teaching that will deliver you from all manner of doubt and perplexity, and enable you to attain unto salvation in both this world and in the next. He, verily, is the Ever-Forgiving, the Most Bountiful.[14]

and again,

The Second Tajallí

is to remain steadfast in the Cause of God – exalted be His glory – and to be unswerving in His love. And this can in no wise be attained except through full recognition of Him; and full recognition cannot be obtained save by faith in the blessed words: 'He doeth whatsoever He willeth.' Whoso tenaciously cleaveth unto this sublime word and drinketh deep from the living waters of utterance which are inherent therein, will be imbued with such a constancy that all the books of the world will be powerless to deter him from the Mother Book. O how glorious is this sublime station, this exalted rank, this ultimate purpose!

O 'Alí Akbar! Consider how abject is the state of the disbelievers. They all give utterance to the words: 'Verily He is to be praised in His deeds and is to be obeyed in His behest.' Nevertheless if We reveal aught which, even to the extent of a needle's eye, runneth counter to their selfish ways and desires, they will disdainfully reject it. Say, none can ever fathom the manifold exigencies of God's consummate wisdom. In truth, were He to pronounce the earth to be heaven, no one hath the right to question His authority. This is that whereunto the Point of the Bayán hath testified in all that was sent down unto Him with truth at the behest of God, He Who hath caused the Dawn to break.[15]

We can therefore rest content and assured that whatever happens to us *is* for the best. Our requirements are to accept and be patient and try to be grateful. Once we have attested in our own experience the truth of the above passages it becomes much easier to be 'thankful in adversity'[16] next time a test or difficulty descends upon us; for then we can say with conviction – and Bahá'u'lláh tells us in these two passages that this is the supreme station to which a believer can aspire – 'God doeth whatsoever He willeth'[17] and 'He shall not be asked of His doings and His might is equal unto all things'.[18] On the other hand, we could say that prayer is the expression of personal relationships: the absolute assurance that our *spiritual* needs will be met – indeed, always are – the laws of the lower kingdoms occasionally giving way to those of the higher, because our Friend loves us. He is transcendent, certainly; but immanence – His close fatherly relationship with each one of us – is also part of Him. As our prayer life develops and unfolds, we become aware, ever more strongly, of both these aspects.

6

Prayer is Always Answered

The most common misconception about prayer is that it is getting God to do what *we* want – to put a rubber stamp, as it were, on what *we* think we need or is best for us: an attempt to secure what we want from God by begging. We look upon God as a supermarket where all we have to do is take our spiritual shopping list and we shall obtain what we want. If we don't, we blame the supermarket for not having the goods in stock. Or we think of Him as a kind of glorified chocolate machine, into which we put our penny (say a prayer) and out comes the chocolate, all neatly wrapped up in beautiful silver paper and quite untouched by hand. If it doesn't deliver the goods, we say it is faulty and isn't working properly. In neither case does it occur to us that our shopping list might be wrong. We are likely to be extremely disappointed if we pray only for what *we* want. This is the main reason why prayers seem to fail.

Many people believe in only a part of God

Many people believe in only a part of God: they believe in His love (by which they really mean His indulgence) but not in His wisdom or will.

We cannot add to God's information about our needs, nor can we increase His good-will towards us. He knows our needs and He already loves us:

Unasked, I have showered upon thee My grace. Unpetitioned, I have fulfilled thy wish. In spite of thy undeserving, I have singled thee out for My richest, My incalculable favours.'[1]

and does He not say that His love is the cause of our being?

Any parent knows that giving the child what he wants all the time and just for the asking, is the best way to spoil that child. Why should we expect our Father God to be different? – and to do for us what we as parents know perfectly well is harmful to our own children? God's wisdom and will are also part of Him.

But we ask for things which the divine wisdom does not desire for us and there is no answer to our prayer . . . We pray, 'O God! make me wealthy!' If this prayer were universally answered, human affairs would be at a standstill. There would be none left to work in the streets, none to till the soil, none to build, none to run the trains . . . The affairs of the world would be interfered with, energies crippled and progress hindered. But whatever we ask for, which is in accord with divine wisdom, God will answer.

For instance, a very feeble patient may ask the doctor to give him food which would be positively dangerous to his life and condition. He may beg for roast meat. The doctor is kind and wise. He knows it would be dangerous to his patient so he refuses to allow it. The doctor is merciful; the patient ignorant. Through the doctor's kindness the patient recovers; his life is saved. Yet the patient may cry out that the doctor is unkind, not good, because he refuses to answer his pleading.

God is merciful. In His mercy He answers the prayers of all His servants when according to His supreme wisdom it is necessary.[2]

Belief in the *whole* of God means that we can open our lives to Him so that He can do in us what He wants to do:

Were any man to ponder in his heart that which the Pen of the Most High hath revealed and to taste of its sweetness, he would, of a certainty, find himself emptied and delivered from his own desires, and utterly subservient to the Will of the Almighty. Happy is the man that hath attained so high a station, and hath not deprived himself of so bountiful a grace.[3]

We should habitually put ourselves into an attitude of willingness to do whatever God wills – habit again! – 'Behold me standing ready to do Thy will and Thy desire, and wishing naught else except Thy good pleasure.'[4] Bahá'u'lláh explains this quite clearly:

O Shaykh, O thou who hast surrendered thy will to God! By self-surrender and perpetual union with God is meant that men should merge their will wholly in the Will of God, and regard their desires as utter nothingness beside His Purpose. Whatsoever the Creator commandeth His creatures to observe, the same must they diligently, and with the utmost joy and eagerness, arise and fulfil. They should in no wise allow their fancy to obscure their judgment, neither should they regard their own imaginings as the voice of the Eternal.[5]

No, definitely *not* a rubber stamp!

As St. Augustine said, 'Love [God] and do what you like.'[6]

Prayer as God's opportunity

So prayer becomes an opportunity for God to do what He wants – what He may well have been trying in vain to do, perhaps for years – in our lives. There is a well-known phrase, one might even call it a slogan, and probably nobody knows who first thought it up: 'Let go and let God.' We hinder Him by all kinds of blockages: our unreadiness, our lack of receptivity, our closed hearts, our unresponsive minds, and by *worrying*. This last is the most common way of showing lack of faith. Do you remember what the Báb said to Mullá Ḥusayn when he was worried about not meeting his brother and his nephew as arranged? – 'Commit them to the care of God.'[7] Closed hearts and unresponsive minds are demonstrated in our arrogant assumption that we can manage our lives without God – pull ourselves up by our own shoe-strings.

We try to put ourselves into the right frame of mind for giving God this opportunity when we say, in the Long Obligatory Prayer, 'O God, my God! Look not upon my hopes and my doings, nay rather look upon Thy will that hath encompassed the heavens and the earth.' Until this prayer is sincere in our hearts, there will be some things that God cannot do through us. He cannot bring in His Kingdom unless we are ready to co-operate. 'Souls who have ushered in new eras of spiritual life have never been content with *working for God*. They made it their ideal to *let God work through them* . . . No one can live with the greater servants of the Kingdom . . . without feeling their power. They are God-possessed.'[8]

Three kinds of answer to prayer

Prayers are *always* answered, let us be sure of that; but it may seem that they are not, if by 'answered' we mean that God granted our requests. So let us examine the reasons for these apparently unanswered prayers. Fosdick gives nine such reasons:[9]

God answers our prayers in ways which either we
    don't expect or don't like.
The replies often come in disguise.
His answer is that we can answer our own request.
We don't give Him time.
Our requests are ignorant.
The form of our petition must be denied so that the
    substance of our desire can be granted.
We make prayer a substitute for intelligence and work.
We aren't ready for the reception of the gift.
We need to prove our spirits by persistent praying.

Let us consider each carefully. The first two can be treated
together. 'Abdu'l-Bahá tells us that 'Verily the Will of
God acts sometimes in a way for which mankind is unable
to find out the reason. The causes and reasons shall
appear.'[10] He tells us to trust in God. Bahá'u'lláh assures
us that 'nothing save that which profiteth them can befall
My loved ones';[11] this leads us on to the idea that 'My
calamity is My providence, outwardly it is fire and
vengeance but inwardly it is light and mercy'.[12] Even the
Manifestation of God Himself is told not to ask for 'that
which will consume Thine heart and the hearts of the
denizens of Paradise . . . It behoveth Thee not to be
acquainted with that which We have veiled from Thee.'[13]

We ask for a *thing* and God gives us wisdom sufficient
to get the thing; or we ask for some quality or virtue that
we need more of and He puts us into a situation where we
can learn to develop that quality. He does not give
anything to us on a plate. A lady I know said that, when
young, she was not a very patient person and she
frequently prayed for patience. God gave her twins. We
need to be alert to this kind of answer all the time.

The answer to our prayer may be 'yes' or 'no' but there is also a third option – 'wait'. The thing we want may be in God's mind to give us, but we have, as it were, to save up for it. Either we or 'they' or 'it' is not yet in the right position. It is rather like a jig-saw puzzle. The picture will not appear until the right bits are in the right places and it sometimes takes a long time to find the 'exactly right' piece to join up with what is there already and complete that part of the picture. Bahá'u'lláh says, 'Blessed are the steadfastly enduring'[14] and again, 'Say: Await ye till God will have changed His favour unto you. Nothing whatsoever escapeth Him.'[15] He, not we, is putting the jig-saw together.

Patience is needed, both with ourselves and with others. We don't receive instant sainthood on signing the declaration card, nor do we tie a label on to our assemblies saying, 'Pure. Made in England.' We must learn to be 'patient under all conditions' and to place our 'whole trust and confidence in God'.[16]

Again, faith doesn't just come to us without effort. We have to acquire it gradually and sometimes painfully. It is as though God says to us, 'You say you believe in Me and trust Me. All right, then prove it.'

Patience is particularly necessary in the teaching field.

We don't ask for the right things: 'Consider the pettiness of men's minds', says Bahá'u'lláh. 'They ask for that which injureth them and cast away the thing that profiteth them. They are, indeed, of those that are far astray',[17] and in the *Hidden Words* He says: 'O Son of Spirit! Ask not of Me that which We desire not for thee, then be content with what We have ordained for thy sake, for this is that which profiteth thee, if therewith thou dost content thyself.'[18]

So, many of our petitions must be denied because it is
kinder:

Know thou, O fruit of My Tree, that the decrees of the
Sovereign Ordainer, as related to fate and predestination, are
of two kinds. Both are to be obeyed and accepted. The one is
irrevocable, the other is, as termed by men, impending. To the
former all must unreservedly submit, inasmuch as it is fixed
and settled. God, however, is able to alter or repeal it. As the
harm that must result from such a change will be greater than if
the decree had remained unaltered, all, therefore, should
willingly acquiesce in what God hath willed and confidently
abide by the same.

The decree that is impending, however, is such that prayer
and entreaty can succeed in averting it.

God grant that thou who art the fruit of My Tree, and they
that are associated with thee, may be shielded from its evil
consequences.[19]

If God granted the form of our petition He might well
deny, by doing so, the substance of our desire:

In one of the most impressive passages in his 'Confessions,' St.
Augustine pictures his mother, Monica, praying all one night,
in a sea-side chapel on the North African coast, that God would
not let her son sail for Italy. She wanted Augustine to be a
Christian. She could not endure losing him from her influence.
If under her care, he still was far from being Christ's, what
would he be in Italy, home of licentiousness and splendour, of
manifold and alluring temptations? And even while she prayed
there passionately for her son's retention at home, he sailed, by
the grace of God, for Italy, where, persuaded by Ambrose, he
became a Christian in the very place from which his mother's
prayers would have kept him. The form of her petition was
denied; the substance of her desire was granted. As St.
Augustine himself puts it: 'Thou, in the depth of Thy counsels,
hearing the main point of her desire, regardest not what she
then asked, that Thou mightest make me what she *ever desired*.'[20]

We often pray when we should, instead, use our brains and work. So often Bahá'u'lláh has to work overtime to get us out of messes we had no need to get ourselves into if we had spent more time on preparation. We may pray to be guided to those souls whom God has prepared for His Cause but if we go and look for them in our goal area on early closing day, it's hardly fair ... Cromwell believed in God as firmly as anyone but his maxim was 'Trust in God and keep your powder dry'.

We may have lessons to learn before we are ready to receive the gift we want: 'The Pen of the Most High is unceasingly calling; and yet, how few are those that have inclined their ear to its voice!'[21] All tests are educative, if we view them in the right light and learn from them the lessons God is trying to teach us. A test is not a test until we see it as such; when we realise that it *is* a test, then we can set about doing something about it. Mamie Seto expresses this very well in her excellent little pamphlet about tests:

By refusing to get the spiritual value from the tests which come to us we leave ourselves open to the same test recurring with greater severity, and we have thereby increased our difficulties instead of decreasing them. God is thorough and perfect in all things, and man is not through with any problem until he has mastered it.

'Abdu'l-Bahá, in answer to a question put to Him on this subject by a pilgrim visiting Him in 1915, replied in the following words: 'The same test comes again in greater degree, until it is shown that a former weakness has become a strength, and the power to overcome evil has been established.'[22]

It may be that we have to prove our spirits by persistent praying before our requests can be answered. You may decide you would like to become a professor of mathematics but it is no use just thinking this is what you would like to be and expecting it to happen. You have to go through a lengthy process of preparation: you start by learning your numbers, then you do simple sums; then you do more complicated sums, and finally, after years and years of steady and persistent progress, you are ready to be given the professorship you wanted all those years ago. It is no use, even if your teacher occasionally seems unhelpful, being spasmodic in your efforts. In the same way, because our petitions seem to fall on deaf ears, we do not have to be spasmodic about them. As Jeremy Taylor put it: 'Our prayers upbraid our spirits when we tamely beg for those things for which we ought to die.'[23] We mentioned earlier that there are some things which only prayer can bring about; and we must be prepared to pray day after day, week after week and maybe year after year for the thing we desire, and be prepared to sacrifice something in our life to obtain it, never giving up hope or losing faith; for if our prayers are for another person, it may be that they are the only link between that person and the mercy and compassion of God.

So in the end it comes down to this: if our lives are in harmony with God, He will answer *us* – that is, our spiritual need – though He may not always assent to our request. He always does answer in one of three ways, 'Yes', 'No', or 'Wait'; and His method is either that He will change the *circumstances*, or He will change *us*.

7

Prayer as Dominant Desire

One of the deepest troubles with our praying is that 'our prayers are often unreal because they do not represent what in our inward hearts we sincerely crave'.[1] It doesn't matter what we say with our lips, it is what we deep-down want in our heart of hearts that we get. For instance, it is no use praying to God to help us to overlook So-and-So's faults and his pain-in-the-neck behaviour at Assembly meetings, if in our heart of hearts we have no intention of overlooking his faults or seeing him in any other light than as a pain in the neck.

We may 'pray against some evil habit in our lives, while at the same time we refuse to give up the practices that make the habit easy, or the companionships in which the habit thrives. We go through the form of entreating God to save us from a sin, but we do not want the answer so keenly as to burn the bridges across which the sin continually comes.'[2]

As Bahá'ís, we do not blame Satan for tempting us but there is an idea which one hears quite often these days and against which we should be on our guard: that it 'had to happen' – a sort of vague fatalism which is only another way of finding a means by which to relieve us of the responsibility for our own actions. Because we either do not see, or do not wish to admit that our actions *are* our own affair, we find a convenient scapegoat.

There is yet another idea which one sometimes hears expressed, that the person expressing it does not feel 'good enough' to serve the Cause, or even to become a Bahá'í. I would like to suggest that this attitude stems, in the first place, from a wrong conception, namely that religion is only for the perfect; and secondly that it is but another way of saying, however unconsciously, that the person does not want to change his habits or modes of behaviour; he thinks he does not need to. There is a part of him which remains withheld from God and is, as yet, shall we say, unhumbled. 'You must take me as I am' is all right up to a point; but we wouldn't make much progress in school if we took that line and refused to learn anything more than we were taught in the kindergarten. Imagine arriving in the 5th or 6th forms thinking one's very juvenile level of knowledge and behaviour was enough! Yet this is precisely what we do, all the time, in our spiritual life, when we refuse to progress beyond the prayers we learned at our mother's knee.

It is, in fact, a very humbling experience to accept God's forgiveness; for we not only have to humble ourselves so completely as not to leave a trace of self in our feelings, we also have to get up and try again – and this can be hard. We are very conscious that people are looking at us and possibly talking about us and to go back amongst them when we know this to be the case takes a lot of courage; but if God is ready to forgive us up to seventy times seven,[3] then we must also be prepared to get up and try again a similar number of times.

A genuine experience of repentance is a very searching and disturbing affair. It is not merely the purely surface regret at having been found out: the 'I'm sorry' of the school-boy caught stealing apples from the farmer's tree, which means nothing and one knows perfectly well that he isn't sorry at all and will do it again as soon as he feels safe and the farmer isn't looking. No, true repentance is far from being such a shallow, meaningless bit of insincerity. Truly to repent implies first and foremost to see our action to have been wrong and then to be struck by the sense of our wrong-doing, to be ashamed and sorry and finally to make a resolve to do battle with it and master it. This is hard; and this is why you hear people say that they cannot pray. What they mean is that they *do not want* to pray, because the effort of really coming to grips with their sin is too demanding and they are at least honest enough to know that to pray for forgiveness when they were not really sorry for their sinning would be hypocrisy.

So for great praying, great character is essential.

What we are talking about here is what Fosdick calls 'prayer as dominant desire, when thought of in this all-inclusive sense of being what is our "demand on life"'. He says, 'Prayer, in this more inclusive sense, is the settled craving of a man's heart, *good or bad*, his inward love and determining desire.'[4] 'Where your treasure is, there will your heart be also.'[5] In this connection, what Bahá'u'lláh wrote to Napoleon III makes the point vividly:

We heard the words thou didst utter . . . We testify that that which wakened thee was not their* cry, but the promptings of thine own passions, for We tested thee, and found thee wanting.[6]

Another example is prayer for world peace. People are

* the oppressed

praying for this all the time but they will not give up their prejudices of race, religion, nation and class which make that world peace impossible. Evelyn Underhill, that great English Christian mystic, says:

Further, we should surely insist more than we commonly do on the close connection between prayer and sacrifice; and plainly denounce that too common type of prayer which asks for results to which those who pray are not prepared to make any real contribution. It is not easy to justify at the bar of reality the prayers for peace and for reunion which are now offered in countless churches, and by numerous individuals who are not in fact prepared to do one difficult thing, or to make a single sacrifice either of possessions or of prejudices, in the interests of peace or of reunion. Peace is very costly, and reunion will be very costly. Both will need great renunciation.[7]

In the sense that we think of prayer as dominant desire, it is true to say that everyone is praying. Their prayers may be worthy or unworthy but they *are* a form of prayer. Therefore, prayer is the inward measure of a person's quality. Nobody can escape dominant desire and so nobody can evade the inevitable measure of his life by his prayer. Let us hope that, as Bahá'ís, we do measure up to Bahá'u'lláh's exalted standard:

They who are the people of God have no ambition except to revive the world, to ennoble its life, and regenerate its peoples. Truthfulness and good-will have, at all times, marked their relations with all men. Their outward conduct is but a reflection of their inward life, and their inward life a mirror of their outward conduct. No veil hideth or obscureth the verities on which their Faith is established. Before the eyes of all men these verities have been laid bare, and can be unmistakably recognized. Their very acts attest the truth of these words.[8]

We can apply this to teaching and winning our goals. Do we *really* want the readjustment to our community life that the introduction of declarants or pioneers inevitably brings, or would we prefer it to remain the nice little cosy club we are used to? What is our dominant desire here?

We can also make supplication a substitute for devotion: prayers, prayer vigils and prayer walks will not have much effect if we don't support our local teaching activities or go personally and look for waiting servants.

The prayer of dominant desire always tends to achieve its object – this is, if one is not totally apathetic, content to sit there twiddling one's thumbs and hoping that God will make it happen. Fosdick points out five things that happen: it gathers up the scattered faculties; it concentrates the mind; it nerves the will; it drives hard towards the issue; it calls eternal forces into alliance.[9] One might summarise this by saying that positive thinking attracts.

Where progress towards achieving our goals, whether quantitative or qualitative, is slow or non-existent, we may with benefit consider this idea of prayer as dominant desire. It could be that not everyone in the community really does want to achieve the goal. Well, they may want to, superficially, but they don't want all the hard work, and sometimes heart-break, that goes with it; and because their dominant desire is to call themselves Bahá'ís without having to pay the full price of that name, there is no fundamental unity of purpose and so the assistance, if not actually cut off, is considerably reduced. 'Abdu'l-Bahá says, in another connection, that the contagion of disease is stronger than the contagion of health,[10] so apathy may win, at least temporarily. It takes a stronger dominant desire to achieve the goal, on the part of the rest of the community, and a determination not to be affected by this attitude, to overcome this situation. Now please do not misunderstand me: I am not saying that this *is* the reason for our slow progress. I am merely suggesting that this element may be part of it and that we should all examine our inner thoughts and feelings and make sure that our dominant desire is to win whatever goals have been assigned to us.

This idea of prayer as dominant desire sheds more light on 'unanswered' prayer. Our outward petition may be denied but our dominant desire – the real prayer of our heart – may very well be answered. Indeed, the controlling passion of our life draws an answer, sometimes with appalling consequences. If you widen this to the world as a whole, you have one very good reason for the present state of the threat of impending calamity of which Bahá'u'lláh warned us. Possibly the most dramatic example of this is His cry,

The promised day is come, the day when tormenting trials will have surged above your heads and beneath your feet, saying, 'Taste ye what your hands have wrought!'[11]

Men cry out for world peace but they continue to seek their own advantage; they discuss abolishing war but they continue to supply arms to other countries; they talk about the brotherhood of man but they continue to discriminate against their brothers of a different race. What kind of desire for world peace is this? If these things are their dominant desires, whatever they may profess, then one can say with truth that the resultant disasters are due to answered prayers.

Insincerity is one of the most notable causes of failure in praying:

Say: Doth it beseem a man while claiming to be a follower of his Lord, the All-Merciful, he should yet in his heart do the very deeds of the Evil One? Nay, it ill beseemeth him, and to this He Who is the Beauty of the All-Glorious will bear Me witness. Would that ye could comprehend it![12]

'Abdu'l-Bahá says:

It is incumbent upon thee to be purely sincere, to turn to the holy kingdom and to generously give the spirit in the cause of the Lord of Might. Verily, this is no other than an eternal and everlasting life which hath no end in the world of existence.[13]

I have quoted St. Augustine several times already but he became a spiritual genius once he gave his life to God. Before that he prayed to be converted – 'but not yet'.[14]

So we see that 'true prayer is the heart, with all its most genuine and worthy desires aflame, rising up to lay hold on God. Prayer is dominant desire, calling God into alliance'.[15] It is only effective if we are willing to pay the price. 'Abdu'l-Bahá says:

The best way to thank God is to love one another.

Mere verbal thanksgiving is without effect. But real thankfulness is a cordial giving of thanks from the heart. When man in response to the favours of God manifests susceptibilities of conscience, the heart is happy, the spirit exhilarated. These spiritual susceptibilities are ideal thanksgiving.

To express his gratitude for the favours of God man must show forth praiseworthy actions. In response to these bestowals he must render good deeds, be self-sacrificing, loving the servants of God, forfeiting even life for them, showing kindness to all the creatures. He must be severed from this world, attracted to the kingdom of Abhá, the face radiant, the tongue eloquent, the ear attentive, striving day and night to attain the good-pleasure of God. Whatsoever he wishes to do must be in harmony with the good-pleasure of God. He must observe and see what is the will of God and act accordingly. There can be no doubt that such commendable deeds are thankfulness for the favours of God.[16]

Great servants of the Kingdom are those of powerful prayer because they are willing to sacrifice anything for their dominant desire, which is to serve God. Think of the Iranian martyrs: they were ordinary people who had no desire to be martyred; but the Faith brings out qualities in you that you didn't know you possessed. Their dominant desire was to serve the Cause and so, when the ultimate sacrifice was demanded, they made it. Pray God we would do the same: greatness of soul is demonstrated in moments of crisis – the descent upon us of trials which we didn't expect.

Prayer thus becomes true and living when it becomes the expression of our most worthy dominant desires: 'The Holy Spirit breathes in this day unto the hearts which are moving, beating, pure and attracted by the love of God.'[17]

8

The Battlefield of Prayer

How do we make progress in trying to conform ourselves to the Divine Standard? It is, in fact, a fight, a continual fight, between the animal and spiritual sides of our natures; and usually the fight is not in the field, where the enemy is ranged before us for all to see and we ride out with all our armour on, the flags flying, the trumpets blaring and horses and men engaged in great and glorious battle – the sort of epic scene so beloved of the film-makers. Much, much more often than this it is the tiny battle within the soul, the one-to-one conflict with only a sword, and sometimes, taken off our guard, with only a blunt or broken dagger; the battle which nobody sees or is even aware of but ourselves and God. The Universal House of Justice has told all Bahá'ís that, though there may be forms of service to the Faith that they cannot render, they all can, amongst other things, 'fight their own spiritual battles'.[1] Prayer is the innermost form of that fight. Bahá'u'lláh says: 'Arise, O people, and, by the power of God's might, resolve to gain the victory over your own selves.'[2]

Notice the language of battle in this paragraph; and notice that we must 'resolve'. Will-power is involved. Resolution is gained in prayer; and then, because we know we need help, it is to be by the power of God's might. You will remember the Guardian's five steps of prayer, which, although from a pilgrim's notes, are considered so helpful and clear, that they have been published for the friends:

After saying to stress the need of more prayers and meditation among the friends, he said to use these five steps if we had a problem of any kind for which we desired a solution or wished help.

First Step. – Pray and meditate about it. Use the prayers of the Manifestations as they have the greatest power. Then remain in the silence of contemplation for a few minutes.

Second Step. – Arrive at a decision and hold this. This decision is usually born during the contemplation. It may seem almost impossible of accomplishment but if it seems to be an answer to a prayer or a way of solving the problem, then immediately take the next step.

Third Step. – Have determination to carry the decision through. Many fail here. The decision, budding into determination, is blighted and instead becomes a wish or a vague longing. When determination is born, immediately take the next step.

Fourth Step. – Have faith and confidence that the power will flow through you, the right way will appear, the door will open, the right thought, the right message, the right principle or the right book will be given you. Have confidence, and the right thing will come to your need. Then, as you rise from prayer, take at once the fifth step.

Fifth Step. – Then, he said, lastly, ACT; Act as though it had all been answered. Then act with tireless, ceaseless energy. And as you act, you, yourself, will become a magnet, which will attract more power to your being, until you become an unobstructed channel for the Divine power to flow through you. Many pray but do not remain for the last half of the first step. Some who meditate arrive at a decision, but fail to hold it. Few have the determination to carry the decision

THE BATTLEFIELD OF PRAYER

through, still fewer have the confidence that the right thing
will come to their need. But how many remember to act as
though it had all been answered? How true are those words
– 'Greater than the prayer is the spirit in which it is uttered'
and greater than the way it is uttered is the spirit in which it
is carried out.[3]

It is in time of need that the lack of spiritual discipline
and fellowship in prayer will tell. If we have acquired self-
discipline and if God has become our 'True Friend', we
shall have the fortitude to endure whatever vicissitudes
fall to our lot in life.

How do we overcome sin, in prayer? Not by con-
centrating on it and taking a morbid interest in our faults
during our times of prayer. We are bidden to bring
ourselves to account each day ere we are summoned to a
reckoning[4] but we aren't told to wallow in sin. One
cannot help wondering if those who do – and there are
some – would love, deep down, to be sinning themselves
but haven't the courage. They take refuge in publishing
diatribes against sin and sinners with such relish that one
can only think, as I did about the author of a book I was
once given to read by a somewhat evangelical friend who
hoped to convert me, 'The lady doth protest too much,
methinks.'[5] The extreme example of this was another
lady who said she had to read unsavoury literature in
order to understand the nature of sin and be able to
combat it better. Such negative proceedings will never
help anyone to cease from sinning.

The human mind cannot contain more than one idea at
a time; it hasn't room for two thoughts at once. The best
way to deal with sin is so to fill one's mind with God that
there isn't room for anything else. By lifting one's
thoughts to God, one's spirit is attracted towards con-

templating the perfections of God; and to contemplate the perfections of God is better than contemplating one's faults! '*Thy* Name is my healing, O my God';[6] not, as I once heard someone misread this prayer, '*My* name is my healing.' Bahá'u'lláh, speaking with the voice of God, tells us that 'Remembrance of Me cleanseth all things from defilement'[7] and so we are bidden to 'remember My days'[8] and 'recall . . . to mind My sorrows'.[9] We are even told to 'unlock . . . the gates of the hearts of men' (and remember, all men are sinners) 'with the keys of the remembrance of Him Who is the Remembrance of God and the Source of wisdom amongst you'.[10]

We should therefore deal with our temptations by means of continual reference to God and the reading of Scripture. No wonder Bahá'u'lláh tells us to immerse ourselves in the ocean of His words![11]

Our struggle is to obtain a clear vision of God's will – and even more to act on it: 'The All-Merciful hath conferred upon man the faculty of vision, and endowed him with the power of hearing', Bahá'u'lláh tells us.[12] 'Success or failure, gain or loss must . . . depend upon man's own exertions.'[13]

As Phillips Brooks exclaimed: 'God's mercy seat is no mere stall set by the vulgar roadside, where every careless passer-by may put an easy hand out to snatch any glittering blessing that catches his eye. It stands in the holiest of holies. We can come to it only through veils and by altars of purification. To enter into it, we must enter into God.'[14]

'Tear asunder, in My Name, the veils that have grievously blinded your vision', Bahá'u'lláh commands us,[15] and this requires effort, for veils, though they are made of thin material, are often surprisingly tough. But 'the greatest bestowal of God to man is the capacity to attain human virtues',[16] and the encouraging thing to know is that we have all got this capacity:

From the exalted source, and out of the essence of His favour and bounty He hath entrusted every created thing with a sign of His knowledge, so that none of His creatures may be deprived of its share in expressing, each according to its capacity and rank, this knowledge. This sign is the mirror of His beauty in the world of creation. The greater the effort exerted for the refinement of this sublime and noble mirror, the more faithfully will it be made to reflect the glory of the names and attributes of God, and reveal the wonders of His signs and knowledge. Every created thing will be enabled (so great is this reflecting power) to reveal the potentialities of its pre-ordained station, will recognize its capacity and limitations, and will testify to the truth that 'He, verily, is God; there is none other God besides Him.' . . . [17]

The demonstration of 'self-sacrifice, courage, indomitable hope and confidence', the Guardian tells us, are what will 'fix the attention of the public'.[18] These depend on moral courage, fortitude, strength in the face of temptation, spiritual poise and a clear vision of God's will – and these may all be won on the battlefield of prayer.

If our dominant desire is to be good, it meets with enemies which must be beaten. 'No man ever became a saint in his sleep.'[19] So our outward conflicts are but an echo of a more inward war.

They who dwell within the tabernacle of God, and are established upon the seats of everlasting glory, will refuse, though they be dying of hunger, to stretch forth their hands and seize unlawfully the property of their neighbour, however vile and worthless he may be.[20]

You will note that Bahá'u'lláh doesn't say *mustn't*, He says they *'will not'* seize unlawfully the property of their neighbours. He is describing the spiritual state of 'those who *dwell within* the Tabernacle of God and are *established* upon the seats of everlasting glory' (italics mine). The inner war for such souls was the getting there in the first place. Their lives demonstrate their state – the fruits of their communion with God. The Guardian tell us that

One thing and only one thing will unfailingly and alone secure the undoubted triumph of this sacred Cause, namely, the extent to which our own inner life and private character mirror forth in their manifold aspects the splendor of those eternal principles proclaimed by Bahá'u'lláh. [21]

One must be aware of the need to turn prayer into action and not stay on one's knees enjoying what the Christian mystics call 'ecstasy' or 'consolations' when one should be attending to some more mundane duty. I once read a poem about a monk who was faced with just such a dilemma. He was in his cell, wrapped in contemplation and in his vision he saw Christ standing in the cell before him. His sense of wonder and ecstasy increased tenfold and then, in the middle of this ecstasy, he remembered that he had to perform some duty which would necessitate his leaving the cell. He was in an agony of indecision, terrified that, if he went away, Christ would not be there when he came back – and he was *so* enjoying his vision! However, after a short struggle, the call of duty became insistent and he responded to it. Having done what he had to do, he returned to his cell in trembling anticipation that the vision would have faded and the cell would be empty. To his great surprise and joy, Christ was still there and as the monk fell to his knees once more in thanksgiving and adoration, He said, 'Hadst thou stayed, I must have fled.'

The story of Martha and Mary in the New Testament[22]

always used to disturb me when I was young. I thought it was so unfair of Christ to chide Martha. She was 'cumbered about with much serving', you remember, while Mary sat at His feet drinking in everything He said and not lifting a finger to help. When Martha complained and asked Christ to tell her to lend a hand, He replied that she had chosen the good part. After I became a Bahá'í I realised the true significance of that story: Martha was treating Christ as a guest for whom she had to make a tremendous fuss and excel herself domestically; she was 'cumbered about' – can't you see all the pots and pans, the stoking of the fire, the heating of the oven, the bringing out of great numbers of plates; 'with much serving' – if you have ever experienced hospitality in the Middle East you will appreciate just how many dishes would be involved. She was flustered, she was hot and she really thought that Mary was amazingly selfish. You can imagine her containing herself for so long; but then she couldn't keep quiet any longer and it burst out. *She* would like to have listened to Christ too but she had to do all this cooking and so on. The point of the story is that all this fuss wasn't necessary. She might never have another opportunity of listening to Christ, let alone have Him in her own home, and it was far more important to come and hear what He had to say than be cumbered about with much serving. A simple plate of sandwiches, as you might say – for in those days they had not been invented – would have been quite enough.

These two stories illustrate the Bahá'í principle of moderation in all things; one should not forget one's obligations, be they material or spiritual!

In this battlefield of prayer, men regain faith and re-establish confidence in God and in themselves:

O My servants! Were ye to discover the hidden, the shoreless oceans of My incorruptible wealth, ye would, of a certainty, esteem as nothing the world, nay the entire creation.[23]

so that, in the end, we can declare with the Founder of our Faith:

Say: My army is My reliance on God; My people, the force of My confidence in Him. My love is My standard, and My companion the remembrance of God, the Sovereign Lord of all, the Most Powerful, the All-Glorious, the Unconditioned.[24]

To some people, the idea of such inward self-conquest may seem impractical. 'Star-gazing' has been used as a slightly derogatory term; but as Fosdick points out, the astronomers, gazing out of their windows at the stars, 'set the clock and made the almanac which measures all our days';[25] and when the telescope was invented, they built observatories and climbed up higher, making their ever more powerful lenses see further and further into the unknown and uncharted skies. They also discovered the Pole Star, by which all direction is set at night when there is no sun to guide the traveller's feet.

In the same way, prayer is an observatory where we may obtain outlooks that orientate our lives aright. Bahá'u'lláh describes His laws as 'the lamps of My loving providence among My servants'.[26] His lamps are hung in the heaven of understanding.

Our wayward appetites are the profoundest trouble in our characters. Bahá'u'lláh knew this only too well and has written a great deal on the subject. 'Thy heart is My home,' He says, 'sanctify it for My descent.'[27]

That the heart is the throne, in which the Revelation of God the All-Merciful is centered, is attested by the holy utterances which We have formerly revealed. Among them is this saying:

'Earth and heaven cannot contain Me; what can alone contain Me is the heart of him that believeth in Me, and is faithful to My cause.' How often hath the human heart, which is the recipient of the light of God and the seat of the revelation of the All-Merciful, erred from Him Who is the Source of that light and the Well Spring of that revelation. It is the waywardness of the heart that removeth it far from God, and condemneth it to remoteness from Him. Those hearts, however, that are aware of His Presence, are close to Him, and are to be regarded as having drawn nigh unto His throne.[28]

and again,

. . . your Lord hath committed the world and the cities thereof to the care of the kings of the earth, and made them the emblems of His own power, by virtue of the sovereignty He hath chosen to bestow upon them. He hath refused to reserve for Himself any share whatever of this world's dominion. To this He Who is Himself the Eternal Truth will testify . . . Open, O people, the city of the human heart with the key of your utterance. Thus have We, according to a pre-ordained measure, prescribed unto you your duty.

By the righteousness of God! The world and its vanities, and its glory, and whatever delights it can offer, are all, in the sight of God, as worthless as, nay, even more contemptible than, dust and ashes. Would that the hearts of men could comprehend it! Cleanse yourselves thoroughly, O people of Bahá, from the defilement of the world, and of all that pertaineth unto it. God Himself beareth Me witness. The things of the earth ill beseem you. Cast them away unto such as may desire them, and fasten your eyes upon this most holy and effulgent Vision.[29]

As God knows the innermost secrets of our hearts, so the deepest need in our characters is right desire – and many prayers express this for us.

Another problem which is a common cause of conflict is, do we wish for the praise of the world or the approval of God? Bahá'u'lláh asks, 'Will not the dread of Divine displeasure, the fear of Him Who hath no peer or equal, arouse you?'[30] and in another passage, He says:

O My servants! Could ye apprehend with what wonders of My munificence and bounty I have willed to entrust your souls, ye would, of a truth, rid yourselves of attachment to all created things, and would gain a true knowledge of your own selves – a knowledge which is the same as the comprehension of Mine own Being. Ye would find yourselves independent of all else but Me, and would perceive, with your inner and outer eye, and as manifest as the revelation of My effulgent Name, the seas of My loving-kindness and bounty moving within you. Suffer not your idle fancies, your evil passions, your insincerity and blindness of heart to dim the luster, or stain the sanctity, of so lofty a station. Ye are even as the bird which soareth, with the full force of its mighty wings and with complete and joyous confidence, through the immensity of the heavens, until, impelled to satisfy its hunger, it turneth longingly to the water and clay of the earth below it, and, having been entrapped in the mesh of its desire, findeth itself impotent to resume its flight to the realms whence it came. Powerless to shake off the burden weighing on its sullied wings, that bird, hitherto an inmate of the heavens, is now forced to seek a dwelling-place upon the dust. Wherefore, O My servants, defile not your wings with the clay of waywardness and vain desires, and suffer them not to be stained with the dust of envy and hate, that ye may not be hindered from soaring in the heavens of My divine knowledge.[31]

One can feel all the poignant love of that appeal, His great, outpouring love for us, His wayward servants – if only we knew! 'Abdu'l-Bahá tells us that 'The indifference and scorn of the world matter not at all, whereas your lives will be of the greatest importance.'[32]

However, it is easier to talk than to act, because sin is usually decked out in attractive clothing and so is hard to combat. For both right and wrong are mostly not abstract propositions and are nearly always brought to us in the shape of a person, however indirectly, and sometimes a friend or one whom we admire and love. In these days of falling moral standards, the insidious arguments of self-interest become increasingly hard to combat unless one has a very clear vision of the Divine Standard. It all sounds so reasonable, so well-advised, surely nobody could argue with that! So we allow ourselves gradually, oh, ever so gradually, to be led in the wrong direction, deceiving ourselves and lulling our consciences into inactivity. No wonder that, in the Dawn Prayer which we often read during the Fast, we pray to be protected 'from them whom Thou hast made to be the manifestations of the Evil Whisperer, who whisper in men's breasts'. *[33]

The Guardian says:

. . . we must reach a spiritual plane where God comes first and great human passions are unable to turn us away from Him. All the time we see people who either through the force of hate or the passionate attachment they have to another person, sacrifice principle or bar themselves from the Path of God . . . [34]

Then you will find people who have 'no time for praying'. They do not understand that prayer is this inward, decisive business of life and that it is supremely

---

* Further references to this subject are to be found in the following places: 'The Evil One is lying in wait . . .' *Gleanings*, p. 94; 'The fierce winds of your disobedience . . . *Gleanings*, p. 167; 'The evil whisperings of the ungodly . . .' *Gleanings*, pp. 324–5; 'The company of the ungodly increaseth sorrow . . .' *Hidden Words*, Persian nos. 56, 57; 'Let thine heart be afraid of none except God . . .' *Gleanings*, p. 322; 'Thine eye is My trust . . .' *Gleanings*, p. 321; 'If ye be seekers after this life . . .' *Gleanings*, p. 126; 'With gold We test Our servants . . .' *Hidden Words*, Arabic no. 55; 'Should a man wish to adorn himself . . .' *Gleanings*, p. 275; '. . . a valley of pure gold . . .' *Gleanings*, pp. 117–18; '. . . the fairest and most comely of women . . .' *Gleanings*, p. 118; 'Set before thine eyes God's unerring balance . . .' *Gleanings*, p. 235; 'Enter into fellowship with the righteous . . .' *Hidden Words* Persian no. 58.

important that they *make* time for it. Without this inward
battle, our decisions are likely to be based on all sorts of
unworthy motives – self-interest, keeping up with the
Joneses, being 'with it' and so on, self-interest usually
being the strongest.

Prayer may be the fight for the power to *see* and the
courage to *do* the will of God but the Manifestation of
God knows that we are weak and need help. God is the
Compassionate, the Merciful. Christ taught His followers
to pray that God would not *lead* them into temptation; but
once they were in evil, to *deliver* them from it because they
weren't strong enough to disentangle themselves from it
on their own. Bahá'u'lláh and 'Abdu'l-Bahá knew this
and many of Their prayers reveal this compassionate
understanding of our frailty: 'I am all weakness . . .';[35] 'I
am poor . . . ';[36] 'Make Thy protection my armoury
. . .',[37] 'Protect me from violent tests . . . ';[38] 'Preserve
me from the suggestions of myself and desire . . . '[39]

There is nothing to be ashamed of in acknowledging
that one is weak, nor in admitting that one has made a
mistake or done something wrong. There is nothing
humiliating in seeking forgiveness of the one wronged
and determining to do better in future. One of the sad
tendencies in modern life is the inability of people to
admit that they might have erred or been weak or
mistaken, and to humbly say, 'I'm sorry, it was my fault.'
It is far more common, unfortunately, for people caught
in some kind of error of judgement or behaviour to wish
to get out of it by 'saving face'. In prayer, we are not
talking about faces, we are talking about our inward souls
which only God sees, and in so far as He is the Compassionate, the Merciful, we do not need to try to save
face before Him. We can't, anyway. As we said earlier,

true repentance can be uncomfortable and we do so need to keep our self-esteem . . . It is much easier to find someone or something to blame. As Eartha Kitt used to sing, 'Everything that I do wrong is someone else's fault.' Well, by not admitting our errors, we may deceive ourselves, but we don't deceive anyone else and certainly not God.

On the other hand, pleasing God and pleasing a friend can be synonymous and we are daily presented with chances of doing both; for just as temptations usually come through people, so also do opportunities to do something for God. In order to love God, we must love His creatures, not simply for their sakes but for God's.

Know ye that I am afraid of none except God. In none but Him have I placed My trust; to none will I cleave but Him, and wish for naught except the thing He hath wished for Me. This, indeed, is My heart's desire, did ye but know it. I have offered up My soul and My body as a sacrifice for God, the Lord of all worlds. Whoso hath known God shall know none but Him, and he that feareth God shall be afraid of no one except Him, though the powers of the whole earth rise up and be arrayed against him. I speak naught except at His bidding, and follow not, through the power of God and His might, except His truth. He, verily, shall recompense the truthful.[40]

9

Unselfishness in Prayer

Our own spiritual needs are, indeed, often brought to our attention by the needs of another. We realize the poverty of our own spiritual life when we have nothing to give. Our spiritual cupboard contains only stones – or at best dry crusts – and sometimes, like Mother Hubbard's, it is bare.

'The object of life to a Bahá'í', the Guardian is reputed to have said, 'is to promote the oneness of mankind.'[1] This also means that 'no man is an island';[2] but when he goes on to say that 'our aim is to create a society which, in turn, will react on the character of the individual',[3] we realise that, far from any one of us being a self-contained unit in the world, our friends are the rest of us: part of us, an extension of ourselves. We not only have to think of God as 'Our Father' in our public acts of worship but in our private prayers as well. 'Abdu'l-Bahá says: 'This is worship: to serve mankind and to minister to the needs of the people.'[4]

The degree to which this social spirit takes possession of us depends on the vividness with which we perceive the ultimate relationships binding all men together: 'The gift of God to this enlightened age', says 'Abdu'l-Bahá, 'is the *knowledge* of the oneness of mankind and the fundamental oneness of religion' (italics mine).[5]

Prayer is the most effective cleanser of personal relationships that there is. People must really be loyal to each other to pray well together. Praying *for* someone is one thing but praying *with* someone is quite another. Prayer for specific people tests the measure of the reality of our love for them. Do we just pray for our family, our neighbour, or our friend and leave it at that? Or do we render them some costly service – costly to ourselves, that is – or give them daily thoughtfulness in little matters? Do we really *care*, or is it just words?

We can pray for ourselves unselfishly if our desire is to sanctify ourselves for the sake of being of service to others: 'It is Our wish and desire that every one of you may become a source of all goodness unto men, and an example of uprightness to mankind', says Bahá'u'lláh. 'Abdu'l-Bahá explains in greater detail what this implies:

Believe thou in God, and keep thine eyes fixed upon the exalted Kingdom; be thou enamoured of the Abhá Beauty; stand thou firm in the Covenant; yearn thou to ascend into the Heaven of the Universal Light. Be thou severed from this world, and reborn through the sweet scents of holiness that blow from the realm of the All-Highest. Be thou a summoner to love, and be thou kind to all the human race. Love thou the children of men and share in their sorrows. Be thou of those who foster peace. Offer thy friendship, be worthy of trust. Be thou a balm to every sore, be thou a medicine for every ill. Bind thou the souls together. Recite thou the verses of guidance. Be engaged in the worship of thy Lord, and rise up to lead the people aright. Loose thy tongue and teach, and let thy face be bright with the fire of God's love. Rest thou not for a moment, seek thou to draw no easeful breath. Thus mayest thou become a sign and symbol of God's love, and a banner of His grace.[7]

Nobody's habits are his private affair. Their consequences run over into the community, be they good or bad. The whole world is involved, if we are members one of another:

When the Scripture says, 'Be sure your sin will find you out,' it does not mean 'will be found out'. It means what it says, 'will find *you* out,' track you down, spoil your character, destroy your happiness, ruin your influence; and because it does that, it will find your friends out, will tend to pull them down with you, will surely make goodness harder for them and within your family circle will load upon those who love you a burden of vicarious suffering. If a man *could* sin privately, he might allow himself the ignoble self-indulgence. But he cannot. Somebody else always is involved. The whole world is involved, for the man has deprived the world of a good life and given it a bad life instead. Sinning, even in its most private forms, is putting poison into the public reservoir, and sooner or later everybody is the worse for the pollution.[8]

It is also true that no man can bear the consequences of his sin *alone*. The sufferings of the Manifestations of God are a universal fact: a symbol of the suffering brought on those Who have done no wrong by those who have:

The Ancient Beauty hath consented to be bound with chains that mankind may be released from its bondage, and hath accepted to be made a prisoner within this most mighty Stronghold that the whole world may attain unto true liberty. He hath drained to its dregs the cup of sorrow, that all the peoples of the earth may attain unto abiding joy, and be filled with gladness. This is of the mercy of your Lord, the Compassionate, the Most Merciful. We have accepted to be abased, O believers in the Unity of God, that ye may be exalted, and have suffered manifold afflictions, that ye might prosper and flourish. He Who hath come to build anew the whole world, behold, how they that have joined partners with God have forced Him to dwell within the most desolate of cities![9]

No wonder that Bahá'u'lláh says, 'The station of absolute self-surrender transcendeth, and will ever remain exalted above, every other station.'[10] Absolute *means* absolute and only the Manifestations of God can attain to this station.

Unselfishness in prayer will have notable effects on the one who prays: it makes the heart ready for service, it gives the imagination to perceive ways of helping those forgotten or neglected, it purges the spirit of vindictive moods, it awakens every gracious and fraternal impulse; so it liberates – it carries a man out of himself.[11]

Another effect is on the person who is the object of our prayers. Knowledge that your friends are praying for you 'is one of the finest and most empowering influences that can surround any man'.[12] Many lives have been kept on an even keel by the knowledge of intercession continually offered for them.

Trust in God and love for men together make for a vital, creative contribution to God's good purposes for us. Bahá'u'lláh exhorts His followers to be 'most loving one to another'[13] and to 'burn away, wholly for the sake of the Well-Beloved, the veil of self with the flame of the undying Fire, and with faces, joyous and beaming with light'[14] to associate with their neighbours. He goes on:

The Word of God hath set the heart of the world afire; how regrettable if ye fail to be enkindled with its flame! Please God, ye will regard this blessed night as the night of unity, will knit your souls together, and resolve to adorn yourselves with the ornament of a goodly and praiseworthy character. Let your principal concern be to rescue the fallen from the slough of impending extinction, and to help him embrace the ancient Faith of God. Your behaviour towards your neighbour should be such as to manifest clearly the signs of the one true God, for ye are the first among men to be re-created by His Spirit, the first to adore and bow the knee before Him, the first to circle round His throne of glory. I swear by Him Who hath caused

Me to reveal whatever hath pleased Him! Ye are better known
to the inmates of the Kingdom on high than ye are known to
your own selves. Think ye these words to be vain and empty?
Would that ye had the power to perceive the things your Lord,
the All-Merciful, doth see – things that attest the excellence of
your rank, that bear witness to the greatness of your worth,
that proclaim the sublimity of your station! God grant that
your desires and unmortified passions may not hinder you
from that which hath been ordained for you.[15]

Prayer for others with this conviction behind it must be
very powerful! – and 'Abdu'l-Bahá assures us that 'who-
soever comes with one good act, God will give him
tenfold. There is no doubt that the living Lord shall assist
and confirm the generous soul.'[16] Again, He says,
'supplication and prayer on behalf of others will surely be
effective. When hearts are united, when faces are turned
towards the Kingdom of Abhá, surely enlightenment
will be the result.'[17]

Such faith in the power of prayer for others could
perhaps be described as 'laying hold on God'.

We are 'members one of another', so, if we believe in
God, we cannot deny the possibility of personal influence,
even at a distance; and if the psychologists try to explain
away this phenomenon in terms of telepathy, thought
transference, or any other mechanism, then we can only
say, how fortunate for psychology to be in line with
prayer and so prove a law of God!

The chief obstacles to intercession are moral ones. If
our dominant desires are selfish, our prayers for others
may be hypocritical. We should ask ourselves, if all our
intellectual stumbling blocks about praying for others
were removed, would we have the spirit that pours itself
out in vicarious praying? Intercession is the result of

generous devotion, not logical analysis. Our unreadiness in this direction is thus seen to be, once more, a reflection of our dominant desire – to remain as we are, or for a quiet life. For the consecrated life sometimes requires sacrificial, not merely unselfish, use of our time and energy, to go and help someone in need when we are tired or when we'd far rather watch the final episode of our favourite TV serial . . . Evelyn Underhill defined consecration as 'faithfulness in overalls' and that is a pretty good description of its implications.

So great praying requires great living and this, in turn, requires great service, culminating, when necessary, in great sacrifice.

When we have sacrificed all our conditions for the divine station of God[18] and are prepared to back up our prayers for others with service, then our prayers will surely be effective! For like the iron in the fire, we take on the qualities of the fire and can pray for others with white-hot confidence, because our sacrifice has made us a channel for God's grace to flow through to others:

If he be kindled with the fire of His love, if he foregoeth all created things, the words he uttereth shall set on fire them that hear him. Verily, thy Lord is the Omniscient, the All-Informed. Happy is the man that hath heard Our voice, and answered Our call. He, in truth, is of them that shall be brought nigh unto Us.[19]

Perhaps such souls are the 'scattering angels of the Almighty', for 'Abdu'l-Bahá says:

The meaning of 'angels' is the confirmations of God and His celestial powers. Likewise angels are blessed beings who have severed all ties with this nether world, have been released from the chains of self and the desires of the flesh, and anchored their hearts to the heavenly realms of the Lord. These are of the

Kingdom, heavenly; these are of God, spiritual; these are revealers of God's abounding grace; these are dawning-points of His spiritual bestowals.[20]

What happens when we pray like this? If we believe that our prayers can 'cause the heart of every righteous man to throb'[21] then this is because his centre of spiritual gravity can change – and when this happens he must take a step forward in order to regain his balance – he must *move*, spiritually.

So a mother, praying for her wayward son, in great love and complete faith in God's goodness, finds her prayers are effective. She joins her prayers with the divine desire, knowing that God must also wish for her son's recovery from sin.

. . . be rejoiced at the glad-tidings of thy Lord and trust in His great gifts, the lights of which have shone forth upon the horizons of hearts and souls, and trust in the assistance of thy Master, and ask what thou wishest of the gifts of thy Lord, the Unconstrained![22]

The prodigal son 'came to himself', we are told,[23] but we can be sure that the most potent force in that recovery was the power of his mother's loving and confident prayers.

When we can pray like this, then truly we can say, not, 'Thy will be changed' but 'Thy will be done!'

References

PART I: PRAYER – MAN'S LINK WITH GOD

1. THE NEED FOR PRAYER

1 'Abdu'l-Bahá, *Some Answered Questions* (Wilmette, Illinois: Bahá'í Publishing Trust, rev. edn 1981), ch. 62, pp. 320–22.
2 Bahá'u'lláh, *The Hidden Words* (London: Bahá'í Publishing Trust, 1966), Arabic no. 3.
3 Genesis 1. 27 (Revised Standard Version).
4 St. John 3.16 (RSV).
5 St. John 1.1 and 14 (RSV).
6 *Hidden Words*, Arabic no. 4.
7 ibid. Arabic no. 8.
8 The Universal House of Justice, Message to the Bahá'ís of the world, March 1981.
9 Shoghi Effendi in *The Importance of Prayer, Meditation and the Devotional Attitude*, compiled by the Research Department of The Universal House of Justice (Oakham: Bahá'í Publishing Trust, 1980), pp. 14–15. (IPMDA)
10 Bahá'u'lláh in IPMDA, p. 3.
11 St. Matthew 13. 45–6 (RSV).
12 Bahá'u'lláh in IPMDA, p. 3.
13 Bahá'u'lláh, Tablet of Aḥmad, found in many Bahá'í prayer books.
14 Bahá'u'lláh in IPMDA, p. 3.
15 Shoghi Effendi in IPMDA, p. 18.
16 *The Letters of Dom John Chapman* (Sheed & Ward, 1946), p. 53.
17 Bahá'u'lláh, *The Kitáb-i-Íqán* (London: Bahá'í Publishing Trust, 1961), p. 152.
18 ibid. also in IPMDA, p. 3.
19 IPMDA, p. 4.
20 *Tablets of Abdul Baha Abbas* (New York: Bahá'í Publishing Committee, 1909–16), Vol. III, p. 645.

21 *Kitáb-i-Aqdas*, quoted by Shoghi Effendi, *God Passes By* (Wilmette, Illinois: Bahá'í Publishing Trust, 1970), p. 154.

22 *Gleanings from the Writings of Bahá'u'lláh* (London: Bahá'í Publishing Trust, 1949), p. 31.

23 'Abdu'l-Bahá, quoted in J. E. Esslemont, *Bahá'u'lláh and the New Era* (London: Bahá'í Publishing Trust, rev. edn 1974), p. 86.

24 *Kitáb-i-Íqán*, pp. 125–6.

25 'Abdu'l-Bahá in IPMDA, p. 13.

26 *Prayers and Meditations by Bahá'u'lláh* (London: Bahá'í Publishing Trust, 1957), no. 176, p. 216.

27 *Selections from the Writings of 'Abdu'l-Bahá* (Haifa: Bahá'í World Centre, 1978), p. 122; also in IPMDA, p. 8.

28 Book of Revelation 1. 7 (Authorised Version).

29 *The Diary of Juliet Thompson* (Los Angeles: Kalimát Press, 1983), pp. 123–4.

30 St. Matthew 13.15 (RSV).

31 *Kitáb-i-Íqán*, p. 4.

32 The Universal House of Justice, Message to the Bahá'ís of the world, March 1981.

33 *Gleanings*, p. 293.

34 'Abdu'l-Bahá in IPMDA, p. 11.

35 *Some Answered Questions*, ch. 46, pp. 177–9.

36 *Hidden Words*, Persian no. 29.

37 'Abdu'l-Bahá in IPMDA, p. 13.

38 *Hidden Words*, Arabic no. 16.

39 From St. Teresa's 'Life'. *Complete Works of St. Teresa of Jesus*, translated and edited by E. Allison Peers (Sheed & Ward, 1950).

40 IPMDA, p. 16.

41 ibid. p. 19.

42 ibid. p. 16.

43 ibid. pp. 18–19.

44 *Bahíyyih Khánum: The Greatest Holy Leaf* (Haifa: Bahá'í World Centre, 1982), p. 55.

45 *Selections*, p. 202.

46 The Báb in IPMDA, pp. 6–7.

47 Bahá'u'lláh, *Hidden Words*, Arabic no. 59.

48 IPMDA, p. 20.

49 ibid. p. 9.

50 ibid. p. 7.

51 ibid. p. 9.

52 In many Bahá'í prayer books.

53 Literally, 'Love and do what you will.' St. Augustine, *Tract on the Epistle of St. John vii.8.*

54 IPMDA, p. 7.

55 ibid. p. 19.

56 Bahá'u'lláh in IPMDA, p. 5.

57 'Abdu'l-Bahá, *Paris Talks* (London: Bahá'í Publishing Trust, 11th edn 1969), p. 174.

58 ibid. p. 176.

59 ibid. p. 175.

60 From 'Degrees of Prayer', in *Collected Papers of Evelyn Underhill*, ed. Lucy Menzies (Longman, Green & Co., 1949), p. 43.

61 'Abdu'l-Bahá, *Paris Talks*, pp. 174–5.

62 ibid. p. 176.

63 IPMDA, p. 17.

64 IPMDA, p. 5.

65 Bahá'u'lláh, *The Seven Valleys and the Four Valleys* (Wilmette, Illinois: Bahá'í Publishing Trust, 1975), p. 36.

66 ibid. p. 41.

67 The Báb, *Selections from the Writings of the Báb* (Haifa: Bahá'í World Centre, 1976), p. 95.

68 IPMDA, p. 19.

69 ibid. p. 8.

70 Quoted by Horace Holley, *Religion for Mankind* (Oxford: George Ronald, 1976), p. 180.

71 IPMDA, p. 9.

2. THE POWER OF PRAYER

1 *Gleanings*, p. 294.

2 *Tablets*, Vol. III, pp. 694–5; quoted in Mabel Hyde Paîne (comp.), *The Divine Art of Living* (Wilmette, Illinois: Bahá'í Publishing Trust, rev. edn 1960), p. 33.

3 *Divine Art of Living*, p. 102.

4 IPMDA, p. 15.

5 *Bahá'í Education*, compiled by the Research Department of The Universal House of Justice (Oakham: Bahá'í Publishing Trust, 1976), p. 26.

6 St. Teresa, 'Life', p. 94.

7 IPMDA, p. 10.

8 ibid.

9 ibid.

10 ibid. p. 17.

11 St. Matthew 11. 30 (RSV).

12 IPMDA, pp. 19–20.

13 ibid. p. 13.

14 ibid. pp. 19–20.

15 ibid. p. 14.

16 ibid.

17 'Abdu'l-Bahá in London (Oakham: Bahá'í Publishing Trust, RP 1982), p. 96.

18 Quoted by Esslemont, New Era, p. 178.

19 IPMDA, p. 6.

20 Tablets, Vol. III, p. 645; see also Bahá'í Prayers (Wilmette, Illinois: Bahá'í Publishing Trust, 1982), p. 65.

21 Tablets, Vol. III, p. 483.

22 Divine Art of Living, pp. 35–6.

3. PRAYER AND ACTION

1 Gleanings, pp. 329–30.

2 St. Matthew 7. 21 (RSV).

3 IPMDA, p. 17.

4 ibid. p. 18.

5 ibid.

6 I Corinthians 5. 31 (Authorised Version).

7 Howard Colby Ives, Portals to Freedom (London: George Ronald, 1967), p. 63.

8 The Practice of the Presence of God, Fourth Conversation.

9 St. Teresa, 'Life', p. 50.

10 ibid. p. 95.

11 Hidden Words, Arabic no. 68.

12 Quoted by the Universal House of Justice in their letter on universal participation, September 1964. Wellspring of Guidance: Messages 1963–1968 (Wilmette, Illinois: Bahá'í Publishing Trust, 1969), p. 37.

PART II: PRAYER AS A LIVING REALITY

1. GOD AS A FRIEND

1 Bahá'u'lláh, Seven Valleys, pp. 5–6.

2 *Confessions*, Book I, Section 1.
3 *Hamlet*, Act I, scene 3.
4 Bahá'u'lláh, *Gleanings*, p. 184.

2. LORD, TEACH US HOW TO PRAY

1 *Tablets*, Vol. I, p. 186.

3. THE PRACTICE OF THE PRESENCE OF GOD

1 Dr H. E. Fosdick, *The Meaning of Prayer* (Fontana, 1960), p. 98.
2 *The Dawn-Breakers: Nabíl's Narrative of the Early Days of the Bahá'í Revelation*, translated and edited by Shoghi Effendi (London: Bahá'í Publishing Trust, 1953), p. 64.
3 St. Matthew 5. 23–4 (RSV).
4 F. L. Hosmer (1840–1929), in *Songs of Praise (1947)*, no. 589.
5 St. John of the Cross, *The Ascent of Mount Carmel*, title of Vol. 2.
6 Bahá'u'lláh, *Hidden Words*, Arabic no. 13.
7 Psalms 46. 10.
8 *Gleanings*, p. 159.

4. CO-OPERATION WITH GOD

1 Bahá'u'lláh, *Gleanings*, p. 85.
2 ibid. p. 65.
3 ibid. p. 140.
4 *Some Answered Questions*, ch. 50, p. 196.
5 *Gleanings*, p. 295.
6 ibid., p. 271.
7 *Hidden Words*, Arabic no. 68.
8 ibid.
9 Quoted by Fosdick, *The Meaning of Prayer*, p. 81.
10 Quoted by Esslemont, *New Era*, pp. 85–6.
11 *Gleanings*, pp. 175–6.

5. PRAYER AND THE REIGN OF LAW

1 *Chambers' 20th Century Dictionary*.
2 *The Meaning of Prayer*, p. 116.
3 ibid.
4 'Abdu'l-Bahá, *Paris Talks*, p. 42.

5 *Gleanings*, p. 219.
6 Quoted by Fosdick, *The Meaning of Prayer*, p. 120.
7 ibid. p. 125.
8 ibid.
9 *Wellspring of Guidance*, pp. 133–4.
10 *Gleanings*, p. 283.
11 'Abdu'l-Bahá, *Selections*, p. 51.
12 Romans 8. 28.
13 Quoted by Shoghi Effendi, *The Advent of Divine Justice* (Wilmette, Illinois: Bahá'í Publishing Trust, 1971), p. 69.
14 *Gleanings*, pp. 86–7.
15 *Tablets of Bahá'u'lláh revealed after the Kitáb-i-Aqdas* (Haifa: Bahá'í World Centre, 1978), p. 51.
16 Bahá'u'lláh, *Gleanings*, p. 284.
17 *Kitáb-i-Íqán* p. 109.
18 *Bahá'í Prayers* (London: Bahá'í Publishing Trust, rev. edn 1975), no. 62.

6. PRAYER IS ALWAYS ANSWERED

1 Bahá'u'lláh, *Gleanings*, p. 321.
2 'Abdu'l-Bahá, in *Divine Art of Living*, pp. 31–2.
3 Bahá'u'lláh, *Gleanings*, p. 342.
4 Bahá'u'lláh, Long Obligatory Prayer, in most Bahá'í prayer books.
5 *Gleanings*, p. 336.
6 see Part I, Ch. 1, n. 53.
7 *The Dawn-Breakers*, p. 39.
8 Fosdick, *The Meaning of Prayer*, pp. 83–4.
9 ibid. pp. 137–51.
10 Quoted by Esslemont, *New Era*, p. 105.
11 Quoted by Shoghi Effendi, *The Advent of Divine Justice*, p. 69.
12 Bahá'u'lláh, *Hidden Words*, Arabic no. 51.
13 Bahá'u'lláh, quoted by Shoghi Effendi, *God Passes By*, pp. 250–51.
14 *Gleanings*, p. 129.
15 ibid. p. 128.
16 ibid. p. 295.
17 ibid. p. 334.
18 Arabic no. 18.
19 Bahá'u'lláh, *Gleanings*, pp. 132–3.
20 Quoted by Fosdick, *The Meaning of Prayer*, p. 147.

21 Bahá'u'lláh, *Gleanings*, p. 195.
22 'The Spiritual Meaning of Adversity' (Wilmette, Illinois: Bahá'í Publishing Committee 1944) pp. 17–18.
23 Quoted by Fosdick, *The Meaning of Prayer*, p. 151.

7. PRAYER AS DOMINANT DESIRE

1 Fosdick, *The Meaning of Prayer*, p. 155.
2 ibid. pp. 155–6.
3 St. Matthew 18. 22 (RSV)
4 Fosdick, *The Meaning of Prayer*, p. 166.
5 St. Matthew 6. 21 (RSV).
6 Quoted by Shoghi Effendi, *The Promised Day Is Come* (Wilmette, Illinois: Bahá'í Publishing Trust, rev. edn 1980), pp. 29–30.
7 Evelyn Underhill, 'The Life of Prayer in the Parish', *Collected Papers*, p. 153.
8 Bahá'u'lláh, *Gleanings*, pp. 269–70.
9 *The Meaning of Prayer*, pp. 169–70.
10 *Some Answered Questions*, ch. 72, p. 254.
11 Quoted by Shoghi Effendi, *The Promised Day Is Come*, p. 1.
12 Bahá'u'lláh, *Gleanings*, p. 274.
13 *Tablets*, Vol. III, p. 620; *The Pattern of Bahá'í Life* (London: Bahá'í Publishing Trust, 1963), p. 19.
14 Literally, 'Give me chastity and continence – but not yet.' St. Augustine, *Confessions*, Book VIII, ch. 7.
15 Fosdick, *The Meaning of Prayer*, p. 173.
16 *Pattern of Bahá'í Life*, pp. 57–8.
17 'Abdu'l-Bahá, *Tablets*, Vol. III, p. 601; *Divine Art of Living*, p. 46.

8. THE BATTLEFIELD OF PRAYER

1 *Wellspring of Guidance*, p. 38.
2 *Gleanings*, p. 93.
3 *Principles of Bahá'í Administration* (London: Bahá'í Publishing Trust, 3rd edn 1973), pp. 90–91.
4 Bahá'u'lláh, *Hidden Words*, Arabic no. 31.
5 *Hamlet*, Act III, scene 2.
6 *Bahá'í Prayers* (London), no. 33.
7 *Gleanings*, p. 293.
8 Tablet of Aḥmad, *Bahá'í Prayers* (London), special section, p. 48, and in most Bahá'í prayer books.

9 *Gleanings 2*, p. 118.
10 ibid. p. 295.
11 ibid. p. 135.
12 ibid. p. 339.
13 ibid. p. 81.
14 Quoted by Fosdick, *The Meaning of Prayer*, p. 185.
15 *Gleanings*, p. 142.
16 'Abdu'l-Bahá, quoted by Marzieh Gail, *The Sheltering Branch* (Oxford: George Ronald, 1959), p. 30.
17 *Gleanings*, p. 261.
18 *Living the Life* (London: Bahá'í Publishing Trust, 1974), p. 17.
19 Quoted by Fosdick, *The Meaning of Prayer*, p. 188.
20 Bahá'u'lláh, *Gleanings*, pp. 297–8.
21 *Wellspring of Guidance*, p. 37.
22 St. Luke 10. 38–42 (RSV).
23 Bahá'u'lláh, *Gleanings*, p. 322.
24 ibid. pp. 37–8.
25 *The Meaning of Prayer*, p. 191.
26 *Kitáb-i-Aqdas*, quoted in *Gleanings*, p. 331.
27 *Hidden Words*, Arabic no. 59.
28 *Gleanings*, p. 185.
29 ibid. pp. 302–3.
30 ibid. p. 97.
31 ibid. pp. 325–6.
32 *Paris Talks*, p. 118.
33 *Bahá'í Prayers* (London), special section, p. 26.
34 *Living the Life*, p. 82.
35 *Bahá'í Prayers* (London), no. 20.
36 ibid. no. 21.
37 ibid. no. 76.
38 ibid. no. 78.
39 ibid. no. 76.
40 Bahá'u'lláh, *Gleanings*, pp. 125–6.

9. UNSELFISHNESS IN PRAYER

1 Quoted by Ruḥíyyih Rabbaní, *The Priceless Pearl* (London: Bahá'í Publishing Trust, 1969), p. 161.
2 John Donne.
3 *The Priceless Pearl*, p. 161.
4 *Paris Talks*, p. 177.

5 *The Bahá'í Revelation* (London: Bahá'í Publishing Trust, 1970), p. 280.

6 *Gleanings*, p. 314.

7 *Selections*, pp. 26–7.

8 Fosdick, *The Meaning of Prayer*, pp. 211–12.

9 Bahá'u'lláh, *Gleanings*, p. 99.

10 ibid. p. 337.

11 Fosdick, *The Meaning of Prayer*, p. 214.

12 ibid.

13 *Gleanings*, p. 315.

14 ibid.

15 ibid. pp. 315–16.

16 *Star of the West* (Chicago: 1910–33. Vols. I–XIV RP Oxford: George Ronald, 1978), Vol. VI, p. 139.

17 *Star of the West*, Vol. VIII, p. 47.

18 *Divine Art of Living*, p. 73.

19 Bahá'u'lláh, *Gleanings*, p. 334.

20 *Selections*, p. 81.

21 Bahá'u'lláh, *Gleanings*, p. 294.

22 'Abdu'l-Bahá, *Tablets*, Vol. I, p. 200.

23 St. Luke 15. 17 (RSV).